THE HEART SŪTRA
Homage to the Bhagavatī Prajñāpāramitā!

Thus have I heard: Once the Blessed One was dwelling in Rājagṛha at Vulture Peak Mountain, together with a great gathering of the sangha of monks and the sangha of bodhisattvas. At that time the Blessed One entered the samādhi that examines the dharmas called "profound illumination." At the same time noble Avalokiteshvara, the bodhisattva mahāsattva contemplating the profound practice of the Prajñāpāramitā saw the five skandhas to be empty in nature.

Then, through the power of the Buddha, venerable Shāriputra said this to noble Avalokiteshvara, the bodhisattva mahāsattva, "How should a son or daughter of noble qualities who wishes to practice the profound Prajñāpāramitā train?

Addressed in this way, noble Avalokiteshvara, the bodhisattva mahāsattva replied to venerable Shāriputra: "O Shāriputra, a son or daughter of noble qualities who wishes to practiced the profound Prajñāpāramitā should regard things in the following way.

The five skandhas should be seen to be completely empty in nature. Form is emptiness. Emptiness is form. Form is none other than emptiness. Emptiness is none other than form. In the same way feeling, conception, mental formations, and consciousness are empty. Thus, Shāriputra, are all dharmas emptiness. They have no characteristics. They are unborn and unceasing; neither impure nor free from impurity. They neither decrease nor increase. Therefore, Shāriputra, emptiness has no form, no feeling, no conception, no mental formations, no consciousness, no eye, no ear, no nose, no tongue, no body, no mind, no matter, no sound, no smell, no taste, no touch, no dharmas; no eye element … no mind element, and no mind consciousness elements; no ignorance, no end of ignorance ... no old age and death, and no end of old age and death. Likewise, there is no suffering, no origin of suffering, no cessation of suffering, no path, no wisdom, no attainment, and no non-attainment.

Therefore, Shāriputra, since bodhisattvas have nothing to attain, they abide in reliance upon Prajñāpāramitā. Without obscurations of mind they have no fear. Completely transcending false views they go to the ultimate of nirvāṇa. All the buddhas of the three times awaken completely to the perfect, unsurpassable enlightenment by relying on the Prajñāpāramitā.

Therefore, the mantra of Prajñāpāramitā is the mantra of great awareness; it is the unsurpassed mantra, the mantra that equalizes whatever is unequal, and the mantra that totally pacifies all suffering. Since it does not deceive, it should be known as truth. The Prajñāpāramitā mantra is uttered thus:

Tadyathā   Om Gate Gate Paragate Parasaṃgate Bodhi Svāhā

Shāriputra, it is in this way that bodhisattva mahāsattvas should train in the profound Prajñāpāramitā.

Then the Blessed One arose from that samādhi and praised noble Avalokiteshvara, the bodhisattva mahāsattva saying: "Good, good, O son of noble qualities! Thus it is, thus it is! One should practice the profound Prajñāpāramitā exactly as you have taught it, and all the Tathāgatas will rejoice!"

When the Blessed One spoke these words, venerable Shāriputra and noble Avalokiteshvara, the bodhisattva mahāsattva together with the whole assembly and the world with its gods, humans, asuras and gandharvas all rejoiced, praising what the Blessed One had said. This concludes the "Sūtra of the Heart of Prajñāpāramitā."

Ceaseless Echoes of The Great Silence

CEASELESS ECHOES
OF
THE GREAT SILENCE

A Commentary on
The Heart Sūtra

Prajñāpāramitā

By
Khenpo Palden Sherab Rinpoche

Translated by
Khenpo Tsewang Dongyal Rinpoche

Sky Dancer Press
Boca Raton, Florida

Ceaseless Echoes of The Great Silence
1993 © Venerable Khenchen Palden Sherab Rinpoche
Second Edition   Printed in 1994

All profits from the sale of this book are donated to The Sarnath Project in
Sarnath, India and Padma Samye Ling in New York State established by
Venerable Khenchen Palden Sherab Rinpoche and Khenpo Tsewang Dongyal
Rinpoche to preserve Tibetan Buddhist teachings of the Nyingma lineage.

Produced in the United States of America
        Printed by L.H. Thompson, Brewer, Maine
        Bound at New Hampshire Bindery, Concord, New Hampshire

ISBN 1-880975-02-5

Published by
Sky Dancer Press
P.O. Box 1830, Boca Raton, FL 33429

THE AUTHENTIC, ESSENTIAL TEACHINGS OF BUDDHA SHĀKYAMUNI,

THE PRAJÑĀPĀRAMITĀ

The Prajñāpāramitā was translated into Tibetan in the eighth century at the time of King Trisong Detsen, Guru Padmasambhava and Shāntarakṣita. Bits of these teachings were translated into the English language in the 20th century. During this time I had the great privilege to give extensive teachings on the Heart Sūtra at the Padmasambhava Buddhist Center in Tennessee.

I'd like to express my thanks to Craig Bialick, Padma Shug Chang, who transcribed the tapes of these teachings; to Phyllis Taylor who, before her passing, gave effort so generously to edit the transcripts together with the assistance of Janet Gyatso; to Judith Cooper, who designed the book in its present beautiful form; to Sharon Raddock; to William Hinman; and finally to all the members of Sky Dancer Press, especially Joan Kaye, Padma Choe Dron who, near the end of the 20th century, brought this splendid edition of Buddha's discourse to completion.

By the dedication of the merit of this auspicious activity, may there be no more war, famine or natural disasters. May all beings understand the meaning of the true nature and attain supreme buddhahood.

CONTENTS

Khenchen Palden Sherab Rinpoche

KHENCHEN PALDEN SHERAB RINPOCHE

The Venerable Lama Khenchen Palden Sherab Rinpoche was born on the eighth day of the fourth month of the Tibetan Lunar calendar in 1941. On the morning of his birth a small snow fell with the flakes in the shape of lotus petals. Among his ancestors were many great scholars, practitioners and tertons. One of his ancestors, Pang Jetsen Tron, was a student of Padmasambhava and was the personal protector of King Trisong Detsen. Another ancestor in the twelfth century, Pang Lodro Tenpa, was the poetry teacher of Long Chenpa.

He was raised in the village of Joephu in the Dhoshul region of Khampa in eastern Tibet near the sacred mountain Jowo Zegyal. The family was semi-nomadic living in the village during the winter and moving with the herds to high mountain pastures where they lived in yak hair tents during the summers. The monastery for the Dhoshul region was called Gochen and his father's family had the hereditary responsibility for administration of the business affairs of the monastery. His grandfather had been both administrator and chantmaster in charge of the ritual ceremonies.

Beginning his education at age four, his father taught him to read. At age six he started learning the chants and ritual ceremonies. At age seven he started studying at the monastery and began ngon dro practice. Later that year he went on his first retreat for one month.

At the age of twelve he went to Riwoche monastery which was one of the oldest and largest monastic institutes in eastern Tibet. Here he was trained to become the next abbot at Gochen. He completed his studies just as the Chinese invasion of Tibet reached that area.

In 1960 he and his family were forced into exile. They left in the middle of winter and were captured and escaped three times during the journey. His sisters died during the escape and his mother died shortly after reaching India. He and his father and his younger brother lived in refugee camps in India. He was eventually appointed to teach at Sanskrit University in Varanasi and was also a founding member of the Institute for Tibetan Higher Studies, where he was head of the Department of Nyingmapa Studies.

In 1980 he made his first trip to America. In 1984 he moved to New York to work closely with H.H. Dudjom Rinpoche, head of the Nyingmapa lineage. In 1985 he founded the Dharma Samudra Publishing Company and has subsequently published a Tibetan edition in eleven volumes of the termas of Tsasum Lingpa. These teachings were held at Gochen monastery which was founded by Tsasum Lingpa. After the Tibetan diaspora he searched through the refugee communities in India, Nepal and Sikkim to locate and assemble these texts.

In 1988 he and his brother, Khenpo Tsewang Dongyal Rinpoche, founded the Padmasambhava Buddhist Center which is incorporated as a nonprofit religious organization. The Padmasambhava Buddhist Center now has chapters in ten cities in the United States, one in Puerto Rico and one in Moscow, Russia. The primary center is located in New York City where he and his brother maintain their permanent residence. Other centers are located in Florida, Tennessee, Maine, Delaware, Illinois, New Mexico, California and Colorado. He has taught in Tibet, India, Nepal, England, France, Belgium, Australia, Canada, Russia, Puerto Rico and throughout the United States

He is the author of six works in the Tibetan language. These include a book of poetry titled *Ornamentation for the Public Ear*, a grammar text called *Explanation of Tibetan Grammar*, two works dealing with philosophy, *Clearly Establishing the Buddha and His Teachings as Without Error through Clear Reasoning*, and *The Essential and Profound Meaning of Madhyamika*, a work on logic, Mādhyamika and tantra entitled, *The Flaming Light of the Sun and the Moon*, and finally a history book called *The History and Life Stories of the Masters of the Late School of Tibetan Buddhism* dealing with the 11th to the 15th centuries.

His works in English include: *The Light of the Dharma*, *The Prajnaparamita*, *The Six Perfections* and a commentary on the Heart Sūtra titled *Ceaseless Echoes of The Great Silence*. He is currently at work on commentaries on dream yoga and ngon dro practice titled *The Dark Red Amulet*. He is also completing an autobiography. His book, *The Flaming Light of the Sun and Moon* is currently being translated by the Nalanda Translation Committee in Boulder, Colorado. *The Light of the Dharma* and *The Prajnaparamita*, *The Six Perfections* have been translated into Spanish and are currently being translated into Russian.

He is also working on building a monastic university on a piece of land near the Deer Park in Sarnath, India. He maintains a travel schedule that includes yearly stops at each of the centers including trips to India, Puerto Rico and Russia.

Khenpo Tsewang Dongyal Rinpoche

KHENPO TSEWANG DONGYAL RINPOCHE

Venerable Lama Khenpo Tsewang Dongyal Rinpoche was born in the Dhoshul region of Kham in eastern Tibet June 10, 1950. Soon after his birth three head lamas from Jadchag monastery, a large monastery three days travel north of his village, came to his home and recognized him as the reincarnation of Khenpo Sherab Khentsye. Khenpo Sherab Khentsye, who had been the former head abbot lama at Gochen monastery, was a renowned scholar and practitioner who lived much of his life in retreat.

Beginning his schooling at the age of five, he entered Gochen monastery. His studies were interrupted by the Chinese invasion and his family's escape to India. In India his father and brother continued his education until he entered the Nyingmapa Monastic School of northern India where he studied until 1967. He then entered Sanskrit University in Varanasi where he received his B.A. degree in 1975. He also attended Nyingmapa University in West Bengal where he received another B.A. and an M.A. in 1977.

In 1987 he was invested with the title Khenpo by H.H. Dudjom Rinpoche. He was later appointed head abbot of the Department of Dharma Studies at the Wishfulfilling Institute in Kathmandu, Nepal where he taught poetry, grammar, philosophy and psychology.

In 1980 he made his first trip to the United States. In 1981 he went to Paris, France at the request of Dudjom Rinpoche where he assumed the responsibilities of abbot of the Dorje Nyingpo Center.

In 1982 he was called back to New York to work with Dudjom Rinpoche at the Yeshe Nyingpo center. He worked at this center until the death of Dudjom Rinpoche in 1987.

In l988 he and his brother founded the Padmasambhava Buddhist Center. Since that time he has served as spiritual director at the various Padmasambhava Centers. He maintains an active travel schedule with his brother and often served as translated for teachings given by Khenpo Palden Sherab Rinpoche. He has taught in Nepal, India, France, Canada, Puerto Rico, Taiwan, Hong Kong, Russia and throughout the United States.

He has written two poetry books: *Ceaseless Waves of Devotion* and *Special Praises and Devotional Breezes to the Accomplished Masters of Tibet.* The latter title deals with the twenty-five original students of Padmasambhava. He has also completed a two-volume cultural and religious history of Tibet titled *Gratitude for and Commemorations to the Early Masters and Dharma Patrons of Tibet,* which was encouraged and appreciated by H.H. Dudjom. This covers the fifth to the ninth centuries and relates how Buddhism came to Tibet. It includes the life stories of the translators and early masters, the politics of the kings and lists of the translations and composed texts from this period.

ༀ༁ བཅོམ་ལྡན་འདས་མ་ཤེས་རབ་ཀྱི་ཕ་རོལ་ཏུ་ཕྱིན་པའི་
སྙིང་པོ་ཞེས་བྱ་བ་བཞུགས་སོ།།

BCOM LDAN 'DAS MA SHES RAB KYI PHA ROL TU PHYIN PA'I SNYING PO
ZHES BYA BA BZHUGS SO

CHOM DEN DE MA SHE RAB CHI PA RÖL TU CHIN PE NYING
PO ZHE JA WA ZHUG SO

ESSENCE
OF
TRANSCENDENT WISDOM

ESSENCE
OF
BHAGAVATI PRAJÑĀPĀRAMITĀ

༄༅། སྨྲ་བསམ་བརྗོད་མེད་ཤེས་རབ་ཕ་རོལ་ཕྱིན།

SMRA BSAM BRJOD MED SHES RAB PHA ROL PHYIN
MA SAM JÖ ME SHE RAB PA RÖL CHIN
Inconceivable, inexpressible, Prajnaparamita,

མ་སྐྱེས་མི་འགག་ནམ་མཁའི་ངོ་བོ་ཉིད།

MA SKYES MI 'GAG NAM MKHA'I NGO BO NYID
MA CHE MI GAG NAM KHE NGO WO NYI
Unborn, unceasing, by nature, like the sky,

སོ་སོ་རང་རིག་ཡེ་ཤེས་སྤྱོད་ཡུལ་བ།

SO SO RANG RIG YE SHES SPYOD YUL BA
SO SO RANG RIG YESHE CHÖ YÜL WA
Experienced by self-reflexive awareness' discerning pristine
cognition;

དུས་གསུམ་རྒྱལ་བའི་ཡུམ་ལ་ཕྱག་འཚལ་ལོ།

DUS GSUM RGYAL BA'I YUM LA PHYAG 'TSHAL LO
DÜ SUM JAL WE YUM LA CHAG TSAL LO
Mother of the victorious ones of the three times, I make
obeisance to you!

།རྒྱ་གར་སྐད་དུ། བྷ་ག་ཝ་ཏི་པྲཛྙཱ་པ་ར་མི་ཏ་ཧྲྀ་ད་ཡ།

In Sanskrit: **BHAGAVATI PRAJNA PARAMITA HRIDAYA**

།བོད་སྐད་དུ། བཅོམ་ལྡན་འདས་མ་ཤེས་རབ་ཀྱི་ཕ་རོལ་ཏུ་ཕྱིན་པའི་སྙིང་པོ།།

In Tibetan: **CHOM DEN DE MA SHE RAB CHI PA RÖL TU
CHIN PE NYING PO**

ༀ། བཅོམ་ལྡན་འདས་མ་ཤེས་རབ་ཀྱི་ཕ་རོལ་ཏུ་ཕྱིན་པ་ལ་ཕྱག་འཚལ་ལོ།

BCOM LDAN 'DAS MA SHES RAB KYI PHA ROL TU PHYIN PA LA PHYAG 'TSHAL LO

CHOM DEN DE MA SHE RAB CHI PA RÖL TU CHIN MA LA CHAG TSAL LO

Homage to the Bhagavati Prajnaparamita!

འདི་སྐད་བདག་གིས་ཐོས་པ་དུས་གཅིག་ན།

'DI SKAD BDAG GIS THOS PA DUS GCIG NA

DI KE DAG GI TÖ PE DÜ CHIG NA

Thus I have heard.

བཅོམ་ལྡན་འདས་རྒྱལ་པོའི་ཁབ་བྱ་རྒོད་ཕུང་པོའི་རི་ལ་དགེ་སློང་གི་དགེ་འདུན་ཆེན་པོ་དང་།

BCOM LDAN 'DAS RGYAL PO'I KHAB BYA RGOD PHUNG POI RI LA DGE SLONG GI DGE 'DUN CHEN PO DANG

CHOM DEN DE JAL PÖ KHAB JA GÖ PUNG PÖ RI LA GE LONG GI GE DÜN CHEN PO DANG

Once the Blessed One was dwelling in Rajagriha at Vulture Peak mountain, together with a great gathering

བྱང་ཆུབ་སེམས་དཔའི་དགེ་འདུན་ཆེན་པོ་དང་ཐབས་གཅིག་ཏུ་བཞུགས་ཏེ།

BYANG CHUB SEMS DPA'I DGE 'DUN CHEN PO DANG THABS GCIG TU BZHUGS TE

JANG CHUB SEM PE GE DÜN CHEN PO DANG TAB CHIG TU ZHUG TE

Of the sangha of monks and the sangha of bodhisattvas.

དེའི་ཚེ་བཅོམ་ལྡན་འདས་ཟབ་མོ་སྣང་བ་ཞེས་བྱ་བའི་ཆོས་ཀྱི་རྣམ་གྲངས་ཀྱི་ཏིང་དེ་འཛིན་ལ་སྙོམས་པར་ཞུགས་སོ།

DE'I TSHE BCOM LDAN 'DAS ZAB MO SNANG BA ZHES BYA BA'I CHOS KYI RNAM GRANGS KYI TING DE 'DZIN LA SNYOMS PAR ZHUGS PA SO

DE TSE CHOM DEN DE ZAB MO NANG WA ZHE JA WE CHÖ CHI NAM DRANG CHI TING NGE DZIN LA NYOM PAR ZHUG SO

At that time the Blessed One entered the samadhi that examines the dharma called "profound illumination."

ༀ། ཡང་དེའི་ཚེ་བྱང་ཆུབ་སེམས་དཔའ་སེམས་དཔའ་ཆེན་པོ་འཕགས་པ་
སྤྱན་རས་གཟིགས་དབང་ཕྱུག་ཤེས་རབ་ཀྱི་ཕ་རོལ་ཏུ་ཕྱིན་པ་ཟབ་མོའི་སྤྱོད་པ་ཉིད་
ལ་རྣམ་པར་བལྟ་ཞིང་ཕུང་པོ་ལྔ་པོ་དེ་དག་ལ་ཡང་རང་བཞིན་གྱི་སྟོང་པར་རྣམ་པར་
བལྟའོ།

YANG DE'I TSHE BYANG CHUB SEMS DPA' SEMS DPA' CHEN PO 'PHAGS PA
SPYAN RAS GZIGS DBANG PYUG SHES RAB KYI PHA ROL TU PHYIN PA ZAB
MO'I SPYOD PA NYID LA RNAM PAR BLTA ZHING PHUNG PO LNGA PO DE
DAG LA YANG RANG BZHIN GYI STONG PAR RNAM PAR BLTA'O

**YANG DE TSE CHANG CHUB SEM PA SEM PA CHEN PO PAG
PA CHEN RE ZIG WANG CHUG SHE RAB CHI PA RÖL TU CHIN
PA ZAB MÖ CHÖ PA NYI LA NAM PAR TA ZHING PUNG PO
NGA PO DE DAG LA YANG RANG ZHIN JI TONG PAR NAM PAR
TAO**

At the same time noble Avalokiteshvara, the bodhisattva
mahasattva, contemplating the profound practice of the
Prajnaparamita saw the five skandhas to be empty in nature.

དེ་ནས་སངས་རྒྱས་ཀྱི་མཐུས་ཚེ་དང་ལྡན་པ་ཤཱ་རིའི་བུས་བྱང་ཆུབ་སེམས་དཔའ་
སེམས་དཔའ་ཆེན་པོ་འཕགས་པ་སྤྱན་རས་གཟིགས་དབང་ཕྱུག་ལ་འདི་སྐད་ཅེས་
སྨྲས་སོ།

DE NAS SANGS RGYAS KYI MTHUS TSHE DANG LDAN PA SH'A RI'I BUS
BYANG CHUB SEMS DPA' SEMS DPA' CHEN PO 'PHAGS PA SPYAN RAS GZIGS
DBANG PHYUG LA 'DI SKAD CES SMRAS SO

**DE NE SANG JE CHI TÜ TSE DANG DEN PA SHA RI BÜ JANG
CHUB SEM PA SEM PA CHEN PO PAG PA CHEN RE ZIG WANG
CHUG LA DI KE CHE ME SO**

Then, through the power of the Buddha, venerable Shariputra
said this to noble Avalokiteshvara, the bodhisattva mahasattva,

༄༅། རིགས་ཀྱི་བུ་འམ་རིགས་ཀྱི་བུ་མོ་གང་ལ་ལ་ཤེས་རབ་ཀྱི་ཕ་རོལ་ཏུ་ ཕྱིན་པ་ཟབ་མོའི་སྤྱོད་པ་སྤྱད་པར་འདོད་པ་དེས་ཇི་ལྟར་བསླབ་པར་བྱ།

RIGS KYI BU 'M RIGS KYI BU MO GANG LA LA SHES RAB KYI PHA ROL TU PHYIN PA ZAB MO'I SPYOD PA SPYAD PAR 'DOD PA DES JI LTAR BSLAB PAR BYA

RIG CHI BU AM RIG CHI BU MO GANG LA LA SHE RAB CHI PA RÖL TU CHIN PA ZAB MÖ CHÖ PA CHE PAR DÖ PA DE JI TAR LAB PAR JA

"How should a son or daughter of noble qualities who wishes to practice the profound Prajnaparamita train?"

དེ་སྐད་ཅེས་སྨྲས་པ་དང་།

DE SKAD CES SMRAS PA DANG

DE KE CHE ME PA DANG

Addressed in this way,

བྱང་ཆུབ་སེམས་དཔའ་སེམས་དཔའ་ཆེན་པོ་འཕགས་པ་སྤྱན་རས་གཟིགས་ དབང་ཕྱུག་གིས་ཚེ་དང་ལྡན་པ་ཤཱ་ར་དྭ་ཏིའི་བུ་ལ་འདི་སྐད་ཅེས་སྨྲས་སོ།

BYANG CHUB SEMS DPA' SEMS DPA' CHEN PO 'PHAGS PA SPYAN RAS GZIGS DBANG PHYUG GIS TSHE DANG LDAN PA SHA' RA DWA TI'I BU LA 'DI SKAD SMRAS SO

CHANG CHUB SEM PA SEM PA CHEN PO PAG PA CHEN RE ZIG WANG CHUG GI TSE DANG DEN PA SHA RA DA TI BU LA DI KE CHE ME SO

Noble Avalokiteshvara, the bodhisattva mahasattva, replied to venerable Shariputra:

༄༅། །ཤཱ་རི་བུ་རིགས་ཀྱི་བུའམ་རིགས་ཀྱི་བུ་མོ་གང་ལ་ལ་ཤེས་རབ་ཀྱི་ཕ་རོལ་ཏུ་ཕྱིན་པ་ཟབ་མོའི་སྤྱོད་པ་སྤྱོད་པར་འདོད་པ་དེས་འདི་ལྟར་རྣམ་པར་བལྟ་བར་བྱ་སྟེ།

SHA' RI BU RIGS KYI BU'M RIGS KYI BU MO GANG LA LA SHES RAB KYI PHA ROL TU PHYIN PA ZAB MO'I SPYAD PA SPYOD PAR 'DOD PA DES 'DI LTAR RNAM PAR BLTA BAR BYA STE

SHA RI BU RIG CHI BUAM RIG CHI BU MO GANG LA LA SHE RAB CHI PA RÖL TU CHIN PA ZAB MÖ CHE PA CHÖ PA CHE PAR DÖ PA DE DI TAR NAM PAR TA WAR JA TE

"O Shariputra, a son or daughter of noble qualities who wishes to practice the profound Prajnaparamita should regard things in the following way:

ཕུང་པོ་ལྔ་པོ་དེ་དག་ཀྱང་རང་བཞིན་གྱིས་སྟོང་པར་ཡང་དག་པར་རྗེས་སུ་བལྟའོ།

PHUNG PO LNGA PO DE DAG KYANG RANG BZHIN GYIS STONG PAR YANG DAG PAR RJES SU BLTA'O

PUNG PO NGA PO DE DAG CHANG RANG ZHIN JI TONG PAR YANG DAG PAR JE SU TA O

The five skandhas should be seen to be completely empty in nature.

གཟུགས་སྟོང་པའོ། སྟོང་པ་ཉིད་གཟུགས་སོ།

GZUGS STONG PA'O   STONG PA NYID GZUGS SO

ZUG TONG PA O   TONG PA NYI ZUG SO

Form is emptiness.   Emptiness is form.

གཟུགས་ལས་ཀྱང་སྟོང་པ་ཉིད་གཞན་མ་ཡིན།

GZUGS LAS KYANG STONG PA NYID GZHAN MA YIN

ZUG LE CHANG TONG PA NYI ZHEN MA YIN

Form is none other than emptiness.

སྟོང་པ་ཉིད་ལས་ཀྱང་གཟུགས་གཞན་མ་ཡིན་ནོ།

STONG PA NYID LAS KYANG GZUGS GZHAN MA YIN NO

TONG PA NYI LE CHANG ZUG ZHEN MA YIN NO

Emptiness is none other than form.

༄༅། །དེ་བཞིན་དུ་ཚོར་བ་དང་། འདུ་ཤེས་དང་།

DE BZHIN DU TSHOR BA DANG 'DU SHES DANG

DE ZHIN DU TSOR WA DANG   DU SHE DANG

In this same way feeling, perception,

འདུ་བྱེད་དང་། རྣམ་པར་ཤེས་པ་རྣམས་སྟོང་པའོ།

'DU BYED DANG RNAM PAR SHES PA RNAMS STONG PA'O

DU JE DANG   NAM PAR SHES PA NAM TONG PAO

Mental formation, and consciousness are empty.

ཤཱ་རིའི་བུ་དེ་ལྟ་བས་ན་ཆོས་ཐམས་ཅད་སྟོང་པ་ཉིད་དེ།

SHA' RI'I BU DE LTA BAS NA CHOS THAMS CAD STONG PA NYID DE

SHA RI BU DE TA WE NA CHÖ TAM CHE TONG PA NYI DE

Thus, Shariputra are all dharmas emptiness.

མཚན་ཉིད་མེད་པ། མ་སྐྱེས་པ། མ་འགགས་པ།

MTSHAN NYID MED PA MA SKYES PA MA 'GAGS PA

TSEN NYI ME PA   MA CHE PA   MA GAG PA

They have no characteristics. They are unborn and unceasing;

དྲི་མ་མེད་པ། དྲི་མ་དང་བྲལ་བ་མེད་པ།

DRI MA MED PA DRI MA DANG DRAL BA MED PA

DRI MA ME PA   DRI MA DANG DRAL WA ME PA

Neither impure nor free from impurity.

བྲི་བ་མེད་པ། གང་བ་མེད་པའོ།

BRI BA MED PA GANG BA MED PA'O

DRI WA ME PA   GANG WA ME PAO

They neither decrease nor increase.

ཤཱ་རིའི་བུ་དེ་ལྟ་བས་ན་སྟོང་པ་ཉིད་ལ་གཟུགས་མེད།

SHA' RI'I BU DE LTA BAS NA STONG PA NYID LA GZUGS MED

SHA RI BU DE TA WE NA TONG PA NYI LA ZUG ME

Therefore, Shariputra, emptiness has no form,

ༀ༔ ཚོར་བ་མེད། འདུ་ཤེས་མེད། འདུ་བྱེད་མེད།

TSHOR BA MED   'DU SHES MED   'DU BYED MED

TSOR WA ME   DU SHE ME   DU JE ME

No feeling, no perception, no mental formations,

རྣམ་པར་ཤེས་པ་མེད། མིག་མེད། རྣ་བ་མེད།

RNAM PAR SHES PA MED   MIG MED   RNAM BA MED

NAM PAR SHE PA ME   MIG ME   NA WA ME

No consciousness, no eye, no ear,

སྣ་མེད། ལྕེ་མེད། ལུས་མེད། ཡིད་མེད།

SNA MED   LCE MED   LUS MED   YID MED

NA ME   CHE ME   LÜ ME   YI ME

No nose, no tongue, no body, no mind,

གཟུགས་མེད། སྒྲ་མེད། དྲི་མེད། རོ་མེད།

GZUGS MED   SGRA MED   DRI MED   RO MED

ZUG ME   DRA ME   DRI ME   RO ME

No appearance, no sound, no smell, no taste,

རེག་བྱ་མེད། ཆོས་མེད་དོ།

REG BYA MED   CHOS MED DO

REG JA ME   CHÖ ME DO

No touch, no dharmas;

མིག་གི་ཁམས་མེད་པ་ནས་ཡིད་ཀྱི་ཁམས་མེད།

MIG GI KHAMS MED PA NAS YID KYI KHAMS MED

MIG GI KHAM ME PA NE YI CHI KHAM ME

No eye element . . . no mind element,

ཡིད་ཀྱི་རྣམ་པར་ཤེས་པའི་ཁམས་ཀྱི་བར་དུ་ཡང་མེད་དོ།

YID KYI RNAM PAR SHES PA'I KHAMS KYI BAR DU YANG MED DO

YI CHI NAM PAR SHE PE KHAM CHI BAR DU YANG ME DO

And no mind consciousness element;

༄༅། མ་རིག་པ་མེད། མ་རིག་པ་ཟད་པ་མེད་པ་ནས།

MA RIG PA MED   MA RIG PA ZAD PA MED PA NAS
MA RIG PA ME   MA RIG PA ZE PA ME PA NE
No ignorance, no end of ignorance . . .

རྒ་ཤི་མེད། རྒ་ཤི་ཟད་པའི་བར་དུ་ཡང་མེད་དོ།

RGA SHI MED   RGA SHI ZAD PA'I BAR DU YANG MED DO
GA SHI ME   GA SHI ZE PE BAR DU YANG ME DO
No old age and death, and no end of old age and death.

དེ་བཞིན་དུ་སྡུག་བསྔལ་བ་དང་།

DE BZHIN DU SDUG BSNGAL BA DANG
DE ZHIN DU DUG NGAL WA DANG
Likewise, there is no suffering,

ཀུན་འབྱུང་བ་དང་། འགོག་པ་དང་།

KUN 'BYUNG BA DANG   'GOG PA DANG
KÜN JUNG WA DANG   GOG PA DANG
No origin of suffering, no cessation of suffering,

ལམ་མེད། ཡེ་ཤེས་མེད།

LAM MED   YE SHES MED
LAM ME   YE SHE ME
No path, no wisdom,

ཐོབ་པ་མེད། མ་ཐོབ་པ་ཡང་མེད་དོ།

THOB PA MED   MA THOB PA YANG MED DO
TOB PA ME   MA TOB PA YANG ME DO
No attainment, and no non-attainment.

ཤཱ་རིའི་བུ་དེ་ལྟ་བས་ན་བྱང་ཆུབ་སེམས་དཔའ་རྣམས་ལ་ཐོབ་པ་མེད་པའི་ཕྱིར།

SHA' RI'I BU DE LTA BAS NA BYANG CHUB SEMS DPA' RNAMS LA THOB PA
MED PA'I PHYIR
**SHA RI BU DE TA WE NA JANG CHUB SEM PA NAM LA TOB
PA ME PE CHIR**
Therefore, Shariputra, since bodhisattvas have nothing to attain

༄༅། །ཤེས་རབ་ཀྱི་ཕ་རོལ་ཏུ་ཕྱིན་པ་ལ་བརྟེན་ཅིང་གནས་ཏེ།

SHES RAB KYI PHA ROL TU PHYIN PA LA BRTEN CING GNAS TE

SHE RAB CHI PA RÖL TU CHIN PA LA TEN CHING NE TE

They abide in reliance upon Prajnaparamita.

སེམས་ལ་སྒྲིབ་པ་མེད་ཅིང་སྐྲག་པ་མེད་དེ།

SEMS LA SGRIB PA MED CING SKRAG PA MED DE

SEM LA DRIB PA ME CHING TRAG PA ME DE

Without obscurations of mind, they have no fear.

ཕྱིན་ཅི་ལོག་ལས་ཤིན་ཏུ་འདས་ནས།

PHYIN CI LOG LAS SHIN TU 'DAS NAS

CHIN CHI LOG LE SHIN TU DE NE

Completely transcending false views

མྱ་ངན་ལས་འདས་པའི་མཐར་ཕྱིན་ཏོ།

MYA NGAN LAS 'DAS PA'I MTHAR PHYIN TO

NYA NGEN LE DE PE TAR CHIN TO

They go to the ultimate of nirvana.

དུས་གསུམ་རྣམ་པར་བཞུགས་པའི་སངས་རྒྱས་ཐམས་ཅད་ཀྱང་ཤེས་རབ་ཀྱི།

DUS GSUM RNAM PAR BZHUGS PA'I SANGS RGYAS THAMS CAD KYANG SHES RAB KYI

DÜ SUM NAM PAR ZHUG PE SANG JE TAM CHE CHANG SHE RAB CHI

All the buddhas of the three times by relying on the Prajnaparamita

ཕ་རོལ་ཏུ་ཕྱིན་པ་འདི་ལ་བརྟེན་ནས།

PHA ROL TU PHYIN PA 'DI LA BRTEN NAS

PA RÖL TU CHIN PA DI LA TEN NE

Awaken completely

༄༅། བླ་ན་མེད་པ་ཡང་དག་པར་རྫོགས་པའི་བྱང་ཆུབ་ཏུ་མངོན་པར་རྫོགས་

པར་སངས་རྒྱས་སོ།

BLA NA MED PA YANG DAG PAR RDZOGS PA'I BYANG CHUB TU MNGON PAR
RDZOGS PAR SANGS RGYAS SO

**LA NA ME PA YANG DAG PAR DZOG PE JANG CHUB TU NGÖN
PAR DZOG PAR SANG JE SO**

To the perfect, unsurpassable enlightenment.

དེ་ལྟ་བས་ན་ཤེས་རབ་ཀྱི་ཕ་རོལ་ཏུ་ཕྱིན་པའི་སྔགས།

DE LTA BAS NA SHES RAB KYI PHA ROL TU PHYIN PA'I SNGAGS

DE TA WE NA SHE RAB CHI PA RÖL TU CHIN PE NGAG

Therefore, the mantra of Prajnaparamita

རིག་པ་ཆེན་པོའི་སྔགས།

RIG PA CHEN PO'I SNGAGS

RIG PA CHEN PÖ NGAG

Is the mantra of great awareness;

བླ་ན་མེད་པའི་སྔགས།

BLA NA MED PA'I SNGAGS

LA NA ME PE NGAG

It is the unsurpassed mantra,

མི་མཉམ་པ་དང་མཉམ་པའི་སྔགས།

MI MNYAM PA DANG MNYAM PA'I SNGAGS

MI NYAM PA DANG NYAM PE NGAG

The mantra that equalizes whatever is unequal,

སྡུག་བསྔལ་ཐམས་ཅད་རབ་ཏུ་ཞི་བར་བྱེད་པའི་སྔགས།

SDUG BSNGAL THAMS CAD RAB DU ZHI BAR BYED PA'I SNGAGS

DUG NGAL TAM CHE RAB DU ZHI WAR JE PE NGAG

And the mantra that totally pacifies all suffering.

༄༅། མི་བརྫུན་པས་ན་བདེན་པར་ཤེས་པར་བྱ་སྟེ།

MI BRDZUN PAS NA BDEN PAR SHES PAR BYA STE
MI DZÜN PE NA DEN PAR SHE PAR JA TE
Since it does not deceive, it should be known as truth.

ཤེས་རབ་ཀྱི་ཕ་རོལ་དུ་ཕྱིན་པའི་སྔགས་སྨྲས་པ།

SHES RAB KYI PHA ROL DU PHYIN PA'I SNGAGS SMRAS PA
SHE RAB CHI PA RÖL DU CHIN PE NGAG ME PA
The Prajnaparamita mantra is uttered thus:

དཔྱད། ཨོཾ་ག་ཏེ་ག་ཏེ་པ་ར་ག་ཏེ་པ་ར་སཾ་ག་ཏེ་བོ་དྷི་སྭཱ་ཧཱ།

TADYATHA   OM GA TE GA TE PA RA GA TE PA RA SAM GA TE BODHI SVA HA

ཤཱ་རིའི་བུ།

SHA' RI'I BU
SHA RI BU
Shariputra,

བྱང་ཆུབ་སེམས་དཔའ་སེམས་དཔའ་ཆེན་པོས་དེ་ལྟར་ཤེས་རབ་ཀྱི་ཕ་རོལ་ཏུ་ཕྱིན་པ་ཟབ་མོ་ལ་བསླབ་པར་བྱའོ།

BYANG CHUB SEMS DPA' SEMS DPA' CHEN POS DE LTAR SHES RAB KYI PHA ROL TU PHYIN PA ZAB MO LA BSLAB PAR BYA'O
JANG CHUB SEM PA SEM PA CHEN PÖ DE TAR SHE RAB CHI PA RÖL TU CHIN PA ZAB MO LA LAB PAR JAO
It is in this way that bodhisattva mahasattvas should train in the profound Prajnaparamita."

དེ་ནས་བཅོམ་ལྡན་འདས་ཏིང་དེ་འཛིན་དེ་ལས་བཞེངས་ཏེ།

DE NAS BCOM LDAN 'DAS TING DE 'DZIN DE LAS BZHENGS TE
DE NE CHOM DEN DE TING NGE DZIN DE LE ZHENG TE
Then the Blessed One arose from that samadhi

༄༅། བྱང་ཆུབ་སེམས་དཔའ་སེམས་དཔའ་ཆེན་པོ་འཕགས་པ་སྤྱན་རས་
གཟིགས་དབང་ཕྱུག་ལ་ལེགས་སོ་ཞེས་བྱ་བ་བྱིན་ནས།

BYANG CHUB SEMS DPA' SEMS DPA' CHEN PO 'PHAGS PA SPYAN RAS GZIGS
DBANG PHYUG LA LEGS SO ZHES BYA BA BYIN NAS

**JANG CHUB SEM PA SEM PA CHEN PO PAG PA CHEN RE ZIG
WANG CHUG LA LEG SO ZHE JA WA JIN NE**

And praised the noble Avalokiteshvara, the bodhisattva
mahasattva, saying:

ལེགས་སོ་ལེགས་སོ།

LEGS SO LEGS SO

LEG SO LEG SO

"Good, good,

རིགས་ཀྱི་བུ་དེ་དེ་བཞིན་ནོ།

RIGS KYI BU DE DE BZHIN NO

RIG CHI BU DE DE ZHIN NO

Oh son of noble qualities! Thus it is!

དེ་དེ་བཞིན་ཏེ།

DE DE BZHIN TE

DE DE ZHIN TE

Thus it is!

ཇི་ལྟར་ཁྱོད་ཀྱིས་བསྟན་པ་དེ་བཞིན་དུ།

JI LTAR KHYOD KYIS BSTAN PA DE BZHIN DU

JI TAR CHÖ CHI TEN PA DE ZHIN DU

Exactly as you have taught it

ཤེས་རབ་ཀྱི་ཕ་རོལ་ཏུ་ཕྱིན་པ་ཟབ་མོ་ལ་སྤྱད་པར་བྱ་སྟེ།

SHES RAB KYI PHA ROL TU PHYIN PA ZAB MO LA SPYAD PAR BYA STE

SHE RAB CHI PA RÖL TU CHIN PA ZAB MO LA CHE PAR JA TE

One should practice the profound Prajnaparamita

༄༅། དེ་བཞིན་གཤེགས་པ་རྣམས་ཀྱང་རྗེས་སུ་ཡི་རང་ངོ་།

DE BZHIN GSHEGS PA RNAMS KYANG RJES SU YI RANG NGO
DE ZHIN SHEG PA NAM CHANG JE SU YI RANG NGO
And all the Tathagatas will rejoice."

བཅོམ་ལྡན་འདས་ཀྱིས་དེ་སྐད་ཅེས་བཀའ་སྩལ་ནས།

BCOM LDAN 'DAS KYIS DE SKAD CES BKA' STSAL NAS
CHOM DEN DE CHI DE KE CHE KA TSAL NE
When the Blessed One spoke these words,

ཚེ་དང་ལྡན་པ་ཤཱ་རིའི་བུ་དང་།

TSHE DANG LDAN PA SHA' RI'I BU DANG
TSE DANG DEN PA SHA RI BU DANG
Venerable Shariputra and

བྱང་ཆུབ་སེམས་དཔའ་སེམས་དཔའ་ཆེན་པོ་འཕགས་པ་སྤྱན་རས་གཟིགས་དབང་
ཕྱུག་དང་།

BYANG CHUB SEMS DPA' SEMS DPA' CHEN PO 'PHAGS PA SPYAN RAS GZIGS
DBANG PHYUG DANG
**JANG CHUB SEM PA SEM PA CHEN PO PAG PA CHEN RE ZIG
WANG CHUG DANG**
Noble Avalokiteshvara, the bodhisattva mahasattva,

ཐམས་ཅད་དང་ལྡན་པའི་འཁོར་དེ་དག་དང་།

THAMS CAD DANG LDAN PA'I 'KHOR DE DAG DANG
TAM CHE DANG DEN PE KHOR DE DAG DANG
Together with the whole assembly and the world with its

ལྷ་དང་། མི་དང་། ལྷ་མ་ཡིན་དང་།

LHA DANG   MI DANG   LHA MA YIN DANG
LHA DANG   MI DANG   LHA MA YIN DANG
Gods, humans, asuras and

༄༅། དྲི་ཟར་བཅས་པའི་འཇིག་རྟེན་ཡི་རང་སྟེ།

DRI ZAR BCAS PA'I 'JIG RTEN YI RANG STE
DRI ZAR CHE PE JIG TEN YI RANG TE
Gandharvas all rejoiced, praising

བཅོམ་ལྡན་འདས་ཀྱིས་གསུངས་པ་ལ་མངོན་པར་བསྟོད་དོ།

BCOM LDAN 'DAS KYIS GSUNGS PA LA MNGON PAR BSTOD DO
CHOM DEN DE CHI SUNG PA LA NGÖN PAR TÖ DO
What the Blessed One had said.

བཅོམ་ལྡན་འདས་མ་ཤེས་རབ་ཀྱི་ཕ་རོལ་ཏུ་ཕྱིན་པའི་སྙིང་པོ་ཞེས་བྱ་བ་ཐེག་པ་ཆེན་
པོའི་མདོ་རྫོགས་སོ།།

BCOM LDAN 'DAS MA SHES RAB KYI PHA ROL TU PHYIN PA'I SNYING PO
ZHES BYA BA THEG PA CHEN PO'I MDO RDZOGS SO
**CHOM DEN DE MA SHE RAB CHI PA RÖL TU CHIN PE NYING
PO ZHE JA WA TEG PA CHEN PÖ DO DZOG SO**
Thus concludes the "Sutra of the Heart of Prajnaparamita."

རྒྱ་གར་གྱི་མཁན་པོ་བི་མ་ལ་མི་ཏྲ་དང་། ལོ་ཙཱ་བ་དགེ་སློང་རིན་ཆེན་སྡེས་བསྒྱུར་ཅིང་། ཞུ་ཆེན་གྱི་
ལོ་ཙཱ་བ་དགེ་སློ་དང་ནམ་མཁའ་ལ་སོགས་པས་ཞུས་ཏེ་གཏན་ལ་ཕབ་པ། དཔལ་བསམ་ཡས་ལྷུན་གྱིས་
གྲུབ་པའི་གཙུག་ལག་ཁང་གི་དགེ་རྒྱས་བྱེ་མ་གླིང་གི་རྩིག་རྡོས་ལ་བྲིས་པ་དང་ཞུས་དག་ལེགས་པར་བགྱིས་
སོ།།

*Under the royal patronship of King Trisong Deutsen in the mid
eighth century, the Tibetan translator (Lotsawa) bhiksu Rinchen
De translated this text into Tibetan with the Indian master
(pandita) Vimalamitra. It was edited by the great Tibetan editor-
translators (lotsawas) Gelo, Namkha and others. This Tibetan
text was copied from the fresco in Gegye Chemaling, one of the
temples of the glorious Samye Vihara.*

༄༅། ན་མོ་བླ་མ་ལ་ཕྱག་འཚལ་ལོ།

NA MO BLA MA LA PHYAG 'TSHAL LO
NA MO LA MA LA CHAG TSAL LO
Namo! Homage to the lama!

སངས་རྒྱས་ལ་ཕྱག་འཚལ་ལོ།

SANGS RGYAS LA PHYAG 'TSHAL LO
SANG JE LA CHAG TSAL LO
Homage to the Buddha!

ཆོས་ལ་ཕྱག་འཚལ་ལོ།

CHOS LA PHYAG 'TSHAL LO
CHÖ LA CHAG TSAL LO
Homage to the dharma!

དགེ་འདུན་ལ་ཕྱག་འཚལ་ལོ།

DGE 'DUN LA PHYAG 'TSHAL LO
GE DÜN LA CHAG TSAL LO
Homage to the sangha!

ཡུམ་ཆེན་མོ་ཤེས་རབ་ཀྱི་ཕ་རོལ་ཏུ་ཕྱིན་པ་ལ་ཕྱག་འཚལ་ལོ།

YUM CHEN MO SHES RAB GYI PHA ROL TU PHYIN LA LA PHYAG 'TSHAL LO
YUM CHEN MO SHE RAB CHI PA RÖL TU CHIN PA LA CHAG TSAL LO
Homage to the great mother, Prajnaparamita!

བདག་གི་བདེན་པའི་ཚིག་རྣམས་འགྲུབ་པར་གྱུར་ཅིག

BDAG GI BDEN PA'I TSHIG RNAMS 'GRUB PAR GYUR CIG
DAG GI DEN PE TSIG NAM DRUP PAR JUR CHIG
May these words of ours come true!

༄༅། ཇི་ལྟར་སྔོན་ལྷའི་དབང་པོ་བརྒྱ་བྱིན་གྱིས་ཤེས་རབ་གྱིས་ཕ་རོལ་ཏུ་ཕྱིན་པའི་དོན་ཟབ་མོ་ཡིད་ལ་བསམས་ཤིང་།

JI STAR SNGON LHA'I DBANG PO BRGYA BYIN GYIS SHES RAB GYIS PHA ROL TU PHYIN PA'I DON ZAB MO YID LA BSAMS SHING

JI TAR NGÖN LHE WANG PO JA JIN JI SHE RAB JI PA RÖL TU CHIN PE DÖN ZAB MO YI LA SAM SHING

Just as, long ago, the king of the gods, Indra, by the power and strength of contemplating the profound meaning of the Prajnaparamita,

ཚིག་ཁ་ཏོན་དུ་བྱས་པ་ལ་བརྟེན་ནས་བདུད་སྡིག་ཅན་ལ་སོགས་པ་མི་མཐུན་པའི་ཕྱོགས་ཐམས་ཅད་ཕྱིར་བཟློག་པ་དེ་བཞིན་དུ།

TSHIG KHA TON DU BYAS PA LA BRTEN NAS BDUD SDIG CAN LA SOGS PA MI MTHUN PA'I PHYOGS THAMS CAD PHYIR BZLOG PA DE BZHIN DU

TSIG KHA TÖN DU JE PA LA TEN NE DÜ DIG CHEN LA SOG PA MI TÜN PE CHOG TAM CHE CHIR DOG PA DE ZHIN DU

And reciting its words, was able to avert all demonic forces of negativity and obstacles,

བདག་གིས་ཀྱང་ཤེས་རབ་ཕ་རོལ་ཏུ་ཕྱིན་པའི་དོན་ཟབ་མོ་ཡིད་ལ་བསམས་ཤིང་ཚིག་ཁ་ཏོན་དུ་བྱས་པ་ལ་བརྟེན་ནས་བདུད་སྡིག་ཅན་ལ་སོགས་པ་མི་མཐུན་པའི་ཕྱོགས་ཐམས་ཅད་ཕྱིར་བཟློག་པར་གྱུར་ཅིག   མེད་པར་གྱུར་ཅིག   ཞི་བར་གྱུར་ཅིག

BDAG GIS KYANG SHES RAB PHA ROL TU PHYIN PA'I DON ZAB MO YID LA BSAMS SHING TSHIG KHA TON DU BYAS PA LA BRTEN NAS BDUD SDIG CAN LA SOGS PA MI MTHUN PA'I PHYOGS THAMS CAD PHYIR BZLOG PAR GYUR CIG MED PAR GYUR CIG ZHI BAR GYUR CIG

DAG GI CHANG SHE RAB PA RÖL TU CHIN PE DÖN ZAB MO YI LA SAM SHING TSIG KHA TÖN DU JE PA LA TEN NE DÜ DIG CHEN LA SOG PA MI TÜN PE CHOG TAM CHE CHIR DOG PAR JUR CHIG ME PAR JUR CHIG ZHI WAR JUR CHIG

So, in the very same way, may we too, through the power and strength of contemplating the profound meaning of the Prajnaparamita, and reciting its words, all the negative influences, may they be annihilated, may they be pacified.

ༀ༔ རབ་ཏུ་ཞི་བར་གྱུར་ཅིག

RAB TU ZHI BAR GYUR CIG
RAB TU ZHI WAR JUR CHIG
May they be completely pacified.

གང་གིས་རྟེན་ཅིང་འབྲེལ་བར་འབྱུང་།

GANG GIS RTEN CING 'BREL BAR 'BYUNG
GANG GI TEN CHING DREL WAR JUNG
Everything that arises interdependently

འགགས་པ་མེད་པ་སྐྱེ་མེད་པ།

'GAGS PA MED PA SKYE MED PA
GAG PA ME PA CHE ME PA
Is unceasing and unborn,

ཆད་པ་མེད་པ་རྟག་མེད་པ།

CHAD PA MED PA RTAG MED PA
CHE PA ME PA TAG ME PA
Neither non-existent nor everlasting,

འོང་བ་མེད་པ་འགྲོ་མེད་པ།

'ONG BA MED PA 'GRO MED PA
ONG WA ME PA DRO ME PA
Neither coming nor going,

ཐ་དད་དོན་མིན་དོན་གཅིག་མིན།

THA DAD DON MIN DON GCIG MIN
TA DE DÖN MIN DÖN CHIG MIN
Neither several in meaning nor with a single meaning,

སྤྲོས་པ་ཉེར་ཞི་ཞི་བསྟན་པ།

SPROS PA NYER ZHI ZHI BSTAN PA
TRÖ PA NYER ZHI ZHI TEN PA
All concepts and duality are pacified.

༄༅། །རྫོགས་པའི་སངས་རྒྱས་སྨྲ་རྣམས་ཀྱི།

RDZOGS PA'I SANGS RGYAS SMRA RNAMS KYI
DZOG PE SANG JE MA NAM CHI
To this teaching, the words of the fully enlightened Buddha,

དམ་པ་དེ་ལ་ཕྱག་འཚལ་ལོ།

DAM PA DE LA PHYAG 'TSHAL LO
DAM PA DE LA CHAG TSAL LO
We pay homage!

རྫོགས་པའི་བྱང་ཆུབ་བསྒྲུབ་པ་ལ།

RDZOGS PA'I BYANG CHUB BSGRUB PA LA
DZOG PE JANG CHUB DRUB PA LA
On the path of attaining complete enlightenment,

ཕྱི་དང་ནང་དུ་འཚེ་བ་ཡི།

PHYI DANG NANG DU 'TSHE BA YI
CHI DANG NANG DU TSE WA YI
May all obstacles, both outer and inner

བར་དུ་གཅོད་པ་ཐམས་ཅད་ཀུན།

BAR DU GCOD PA THAMS CAD KUN
BAR DU CHÖ PA TAM CHE KÜN
To our attaining complete enlightenment

ཉེ་བར་ཞི་བར་མཛད་དུ་གསོལ།

NYE BAR ZHI BAR MDZAD DU GSOL
NYE WAR ZHI WAR DZE DU SÖL
Be totally pacified!

Prajñāpāramitā

HOMAGE

All phenomenal existents are primordially free from all complexities and the four extremes, and are uncompounded, profound, and in the clear light state. This is the basic mother.

The great activity is the unfocused compassion of the four immeasurables, combined with the six pāramitās in supreme bodhicitta. This is the mother of the application of the path.

The possession of the two purities is free from attachments, blockage, ignorance and emotional obscurations. The primordial wisdom self-awareness is the result mother.

Great Prajñāpāramitā, the supreme mother of the four noble children of the three times and ten directions, may you always be victorious in the hearts of beings!

COMMITMENT

I will echo the ceaseless voice of the great Shakya Singhe supreme teacher of the three realms, who by his teaching of the Prajñāpāramita, will subdue the noise of intellectual jackals holding extreme views.

ASPIRATION

The sharp primordial wisdom eye of non-grasping is developed through knowledge of discriminating awareness. Thus arises the vajra of the union of emptiness and appearance.

May everyone achieve the dharmakāya of great equanimity.

INTRODUCTION

I bow to Prajñāpāramitā, the Wisdom Gone Beyond!

These days, throughout the world and especially in this powerful nation of America, it is common to see, even daily, developments in the fields of science which are increasing the general understanding of how matter actually exists and functions, from the external point of view. These scientists deserve continuous praise for their analyses of actualities' manner of existence; regardless of whether or not they believe in the Buddha, their work has proved much that accords with his teachings. However, science alone has not proved itself able to dispel suffering and produce blissful experiences in any ultimate way.

To achieve such ultimate results, it is necessary to look inward to the vast, exceedingly profound mind itself, and discover its mode of being. Since this is not easily done—in fact it is extremely difficult—one generally needs to find and follow a flawless path. The Prajñāpāramitā is such a path. Through steady reliance on its perfect view, it is possible to dispel all suffering and produce all kinds of benefit and happiness for both self and others, as did innumerable scholar-practitioners who appeared and were witnessed in ancient India and Tibet. The view they attained is like the sky, free of conceptual extremes; it is like the sun, clearing away the dark clouds of ignorance; and it is like the moon, emitting cool rays of calm and bliss. When necessary, it can be sharp, like an axe, chopping down the poison tree of egotism. It can be like a harsh wind, scattering all concepts, sorrows, and adverse circumstances. Like a crashing wave, it can wash away all habitual traces and grime. Like a fireball, it can incinerate impurities from the hundreds of emotional attachments. It is a ground capable of supporting freedom and omniscience, and a primordial mother, giving birth to the enlightened ones. In short, it is like a single medicine for a hundred ills, curing the degenerative diseases of the eight worldly cares. If one understands this perfect view, then faith, compassion, wisdom, meditative experiences, goodness, beauty, and insurpassable qualities will arise spontaneously in one's mind, just as flowers and trees grow in springtime without effort.

Presently in this world, those people are rare indeed who are seeking knowledge from the inner perspective, where the experience of mind's meaning itself—its profound and vast mode of being—can be developed and increased. Therefore I felt it necessary to arouse an especially strong, positive attitude to compose this brief exposition on the *Prajñāpāramitā*, so that the hundred-fold grasping at terrifying projections, in darkness of stupidity, may be liberated right where it is, and so that all beings may attain stability within the expanse of the absolute wisdom which is their own, individual awareness.

My own education began when I entered the great college at Do-Kham Riwoche Drukpa Khang (*mDo-khams Ri-bo-che 'Brug-pa-khang*) called Do-Ngak Shedrub Pelgye Ling (*mDo-sngags bShad-sgrub 'Phel-rgyas Gling*). At first my behavior was wild, despite very strict rules. I was far away from home, and poor in supplies and clothing. I did not study, and failed the first examination. My teacher, the Khen Rinpoche, kindly and frequently offered his advice, but I did not listen until I was harshly criticized and punished by the Dharma disciplinarian. After that day, I recognized my faults. I began to listen and think without break, studying even at night by moonlight and, when the moon was gone, by the light of a burning stick of incense. Thus studying the great root and commentarial texts with care and diligence, I earned the praise of my teacher and the reputation of being the smartest among my peers. Khen Rinpoche poured over me all the teachings of the Victorious One, both the general and the particular, the holy treasures of the lineage masters, and the nectar-like instructions from the most secret long transmission of the Old Translation School. These latter included the teachings of the two omniscient ones, Rongzom and Longchenpa, and the pointing out instructions according to the texts of Jamgon Mipham. I, Palden Sherab, well attained all that.

When the Red Chinese barbarians came to destroy the Buddha's teachings and the culture of Tibet, I decided to leave. I gave away my every last possession, offered a communal tea, and, in front of Khen Rinpoche, offered a mandala as a prayer for his long life. On the night of my departure I went to see Rinpoche to offer a last white scarf. My heart was exceedingly sad. "Don't stay here," I pleaded, "please go to Padma Kö." "I won't be able to reach Padma Kö," he said. I pleaded again, but he replied in the same way. I continued to weep and plead, and he said, "Okay, okay, now don't cry. I'll pray that I'll be able to get to Padma Kö! But anyway you go. You will get to Padma Kö and India. No matter what karma you meet with, don't turn your mind away from the Three Precious Jewels. Now, you know that your learning is good. Therefore you will definitely benefit both teachings and beings. Don't mess up! Keep this is in your mind."

It was 1961 when I arrived in India. On the way, I had encountered great difficulties, exhaustion and danger, but I always held his words closely in my mind. To those Indian, Nepalese, Tibetan, and other peoples having faith in and connections with me, I have taught whatever Tibetan Dharma and culture I know. For seventeen years I taught in Varanasi at the Tibetan Institute for

Higher Studies where the number of good students—through whom both teachings and beings could benefit—was not small.

In 1980, I left India and came to wander in the Western continents. The inner teachings of Tibetan Dharma had begun to spread about twenty years previously, and I found men and women of great intelligence and faith, such that lamas both great and small who have come here to teach have been kept very busy giving Vajrayāna empowerments and transmissions, as well as profound instructions. However, expositions on the sutraic and tantric traditions of the Prajñāpāramitā, which is the very heart of the Dharma, have been too few. I think the lot must have fallen upon me to make a contribution on this subject. Therefore it is with much pleasure and an intention to help that I present the following exegesis, which represents a mere handful of water out of what is like an ocean of the *Prajñāpāramitā* teachings. Based on talks I gave at my Dharma centers in Florida and Tennessee, it presents the path that all sentient beings might follow towards the pure light of their innermost wisdom.

I myself am ordinary, the smallest of the small. But the teachings of the Prajñāpāramitā lineage contained in my mind are not ordinary or small. They are the pronouncement of the pure beings, the good, great, rarefied stream of the nectar of deathlessness.

This straightforward introduction was written by myself, Palden Sherab, who holds the title of a Nyingmapa abbot, in the seventh month of the Western year 1991, on Florida's "Eastern Ocean Beach Lined With a Rosary of Palms," at Padmasambhava Center, in Mandarava's Temple.

PRAJÑĀPĀRAMITĀ AND *THE HEART SŪTRA*

A Commentary by Khenchen Palden Sherab Rinpoche
Translated by Khenpo Tsewang Dongyal Rinpoche

What is the nature of Prajñāpāramitā? It is the wisdom that realizes directly phenomena as they are: a wisdom free from extremes, having gone to, or in the process of going to, the "other shore," beyond all abiding in any particular position. The Sanskrit term Prajñāpāramitā is translated many ways: for example, "supreme transcendent wisdom," "the great emptiness," "the true nature of all phenomena," or "the absolute truth." All these names refer to the ultimate level of every teaching given by Buddha Shākyamuni. It is the profound essence of the Mahāyāna, and in the Vajrayāna it is the very basis of every practice. It is therefore important that we who have entered the path and begun Vajrayāna training acquire some depth and subtlety in our understanding of Prajñāpāramitā. I am going to give you an explanation of its meaning within the lines of the *Heart Sūtra*. Let us try to listen joyfully and diligently, applying what we hear with our ears to the depths of our minds and hearts. First, I will give you some general background of the text.

BACKGROUND

Prajñāpāramitā also refers to a large body of teachings with many levels and categories. Lord Buddha is said to have taught one hundred million stanzas in the nāga[1] realms, as well as many hundreds of stanzas in this human realm—specifically, in Magadha, India, on Vulture Peak, to countless arhats and bodhisattvas. At first the teachings were compiled by the bodhisattvas Mañjushrī, Maitreya, and Avalokiteshvara, among others. Then, many great masters, such as Nāgārjuna, Asaṅga, Āryadeva, Vasubandhu, Dignāga, Dharma-kīrti, Ārya Vimuktisena, Haribhadra, and Shāntarakṣita, wrote commentaries according to their understanding, based on two principal schools of interpretation: the Mahāyāna Cittamātra and the Mādhyamika. The *Prajñāpāramitā* teachings were transmitted in an unbroken line of masters, whose followers, more numerous than in any other place and time, were able to realize the pure mode of being of the most profound state of mind. Due to their attainment of the exalted level of unsurpassable calm and bliss, their country, India, became known in Tibet as the "exalted land."

These profound teachings reached Tibet in the eighth century, when the great Dharma King Trisong Detsen (*Khri-srong lDe'u-btsan*), together with Guru Padmasambhava and the Abbot Shāntarakṣita, were laying the foundation of Buddhism in the Snow Mountains. They built and founded Samye Monastery, named in full "Enduring, Spontaneously Arisen Samye," the first great non-sectarian institution in Tibet to rival India's Nālandā. With its blend of three architectural styles from Tibet, India, and China, and its configuration as a sacred mandala, Samye's rise and eventual destruction by the Chinese became indicators for the fate of the Buddha's teachings in Tibet. Having built Samye, the King set in motion his plan to import and translate all the teachings of the

---

[1] Human above the waist and serpent below, these powerful beings, belonging to both human and god realms, inhabit bodies of water or swampy areas. In their jewelled subterranean kingdoms they are said to be guardians of wisdom. It is from the nāga realms that Nāgārjuna received the teachings for the Mādhyamika philosophy he developed.

Buddha. To this end he invited to Samye's great temple hall 500 great pandits, of whom the foremost was Vimalamitra; in addition, there were 108 realized masters who were like buddhas; 108 great translators including Vairocana and the trio of Kawa Paltsek (*sKaba dPal-tshegs*), Chogro Lu Gyaltsen (*Cog-ro Klu'i rGyal-mtshan*), and Zhang Yeshe De (*Zhang Ye-shes sDe*); and 1008 secondary translators. Their methods of translation were extremely thorough. Whether translating Hīnayāna or Dzogchen, each master would be accompanied by at least one other qualified scholar. It was the custom—even for such great masters as Vimalamitra and Rinchen-De—to first pay homage to the Three Jewels and then to contemplate very deeply on the meanings before setting pen to paper. The resulting translations were accurate and true.

After bringing in whatever Prajñāpāramitā texts were extant in India, the King sent the Tibetan translator Lang Khampa Gocha (*rLangs Khams-pa Go-cha*) to India to memorize the complete 100,000 stanzas, return to Tibet, and then translate them. That copy was written with a mixture of the Dharma King's nose-blood and the milk of a white goat, and was known as the "Red Document," or the "Smaller Lord's Translation." A second copy was made under similar circumstances by the Tibetan translators Wä (*dBas*) Mañjushrī and Nyang (*Myang*) Indravaro, with a mixture of some singed hair from the King's head, and the milk of a white goat. It was called the "Blue Document," and was checked by the great translator Vairocana, who corrected errors in organization, added missing verses and filled out abbreviations. This felicitous translation was written out in the great translator's own hand, and named for the "100,000 Deer Case" in which it was kept. It was also called the "Medium Lord's Translation." Eventually, during the lifetime of the Dharma King's grandson, Master Tri Ralpachen (*Khri Ral-pacan*), a "Large Lord's Translation," divided into seventeen sections, was composed by the scholar Paṇḍita Surendrabodhi and the translator Kachog (*sKa-cog*).

In this way, during the time of the Old School, all the root Prajñāpāramitā scriptures were translated into Tibetan, where they became famous as the "Seventeen Mother and Son Prajñā-pāramitā" texts. The commentaries written earlier by the great Indian masters, of which the principal one is the Abhisamayā-laṃkāra, also were translated by both Old and New Schools, and became the "Twenty-One Vast Prajñāpāramitā Commentaries." Thus all the Prajñāpāramitā scriptures and commentaries are preserved intact in the Kangyur (*bKa'-'gyur*) and Tangyur (*bsTan-'gyur*), the Tibetan canon.

TIBETAN LINEAGE

The Tibetan lineage of the Prajñāpāramitā teachings continued through the transition from the Nyingma to the Sarma schools. During the time of the New School, The Great Translator of Ngog (*rNgog*), Loden Sherab (*bLo-ldan Shes-rab*), established a tradition of teaching, debating and composing Buddhist theory at the glorious Dharma college of Sangpu Netog (*gSang-phu Ne'u-thog*), which was like Vikramashīlā college in India and had been built by Ngog Legpa Sherab (*rNgog Legs-pa'i Shes-rab*), inspired by the great scholar Atīsha. Of his illustrious students, numerous as the stars crowding the sky, it was a spiritual son named Rechen Sherab Bar (*Bre-chen Shes-rab 'Bar*) who fused the Prajñāpāramitā exegetical tradition of the Old and New Schools. After him came Ar Changchub Öd (*Ar Byang-chub 'Od*), then Khur Shertsön (*Sher-brtson*), Karchung Ringmo (*dKar-chung Ring-mo*), Zhang Yelpa Mönlam Tsultrim (*gYel-pa sMon-lam Tshul-khrims*), Nyalzigpa Sherab Lodrö (*gNyal-zhig-pa Shes-rab Blo-gros*), Gyaching Rupa (*rGya-mching Ru-pa*), Chumigpa Senge Pal (*Chu-mig-pa Senge dPal*), Lhodragpa (*Lho-brag-pa*), Tsengonpa (*bTsan-dgon-pa*), Wen (*dBen*) and Ge (*dGe*), Ladrangpa (*Bla-brang-pa*), the second Chödrag (*Chos-brags*), and then Longchen Rabjam (*Klong-chen Rab-'byams*).

Again, after Lhodragpa (*Lho-brag-pa*) came Tseme Kyebu (*Tshad-ma'i sKyes-bu*), Butön Rinchen Drub (*Bu-ston Rin-chen Grub*), and Yatrug (*gYag-phrug*), after whom came both Yatön (*gYag-ston*) and Redapa (*Red-mda'-pa*). Yatön's student was Rongtön (*Rong-ston*), Redapa's student was the Venerable Great Tsong-khapa. Their tradition of exegesis gradually came down to Minling Lochen (*sMin-gling Lo-chen*) Dharmashrī and Padma Gyurme Gyatso (*'Gyur-med rGya-rtsho*). These and many other lineages eventually came down to Gyalse Shenpen Thaye (*rGyal-sras gZhan-pan mTha-yas*), Patrul (*dPal-sprul*) Rinpoche, Jamgon Kongtrul (*'Jam-dgon Kong-sprul*), and Jamyang Khyentse Wangpo (*'Jam-dbyangs mKhyen-brtse'i dBang-po*). Their principal disciple was Jamgon Mipham (*'Jam-dgon Mi-pham*), whose lineage was transmitted to Khenchen Zhenga (*mKhan-chen gZhan-dga'*). From him, the lineage went to Mipham Rinpoche's student Sechen Gyaltsab Padma Namgyal (*Zhe-chen rGyal-tshab Padma rNam-rgyal*), Khenchen Kunzang Palden (*mKhan-chen Kun-bzang dPal-ldan*) and so forth. Their successors were Kathog Khenpo Legse Jorden (*Kaḥ-thog mKhan-po Legs-bshad 'Byor-ldan*), Kathog Khenpo Nüden (*Nus-ldan*), Kathog Khenpo Aksu, and finally my root guru, the great scholar-practitioner Kathog Khenpo A-she (*A-shad*), also known as Khewang Tendzin Dragpa (*mKhas-dbang bsTan-'dzin Grags-pa*) Rinpoche.

CAPTIONS TO COLOR PLATES

Frontispiece. Ancient statue from east India known as the Gyakar Sharli. Brought to Tibet in the 8th century. Tibetan historical texts agree that it was crafted in the second or third century A.D. Some believe it originates from the time of Shākyamuni Buddha himself and was blessed by him.

1. Gold ink piece of the page of the Prajñāpāramitā. The entire text was penned in gold ink on blue paper and was held as a treasure in Riwoche monastery. Padma Tso, a fifteenth century ḍākinī emanation of Yeshe Tsogyal, left the life of a householder to become a wandering yogini in the central area of eastern Tibet—Riwoche and Do Shul. Many of the old families in this areas still have her relics as part of their family treasures. Lamas requested gold of her for this text and many others and she produced it by transforming her secret water into that element. After the communist Chinese destruction, only a few fragments such as this one survived, secretly preserved by devoted students.

2. The Prajñāpāramitā in Fifty Stanzas. Sanskrit on palm leaf pages. This is a treasure from the library at Samye. Texts such as these were brought from India to Tibet during the eighth and ninth centuries. They were carried around the bodies of the great Indian masters and translators. Shown half-size.

3. First page of the *Sañcaygāthā*, the Condensed Verses of the Prajñāpāramitā taught by the Buddha Shākyamuni himself. This is a leading example of a rare teaching style, a continuous presentation rather than a dialogue. The detail picture is Prajñāpāramitā, the mother of the buddhas. This is part of a complete illuminated Tibetan manuscript *Prajñāpāramitā Sūtra*. The text is comprised of 74 folios, gold and silver on blue paper. Dimensions: 14" x 4.5" (35.5 cm x 11.5 cm) Tibet 12th C. *Courtesy of Mokotoff Asian Arts*

4. Detail shows Prajñāpāramita, mother of all buddhas.

Calligraphy on the endleaves is the Mantra of Interdependent Coordination, written in ancient Sanskrit Lenza letters by Ven. Khenchen Palden Sherab Rinpoche.

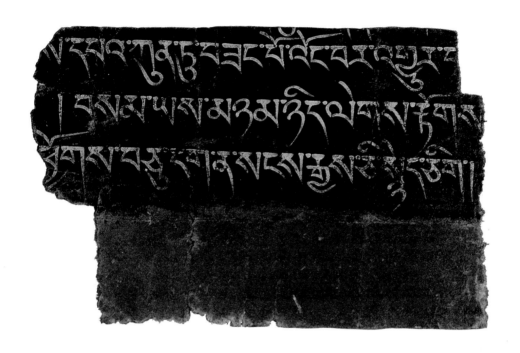

PLATE 1

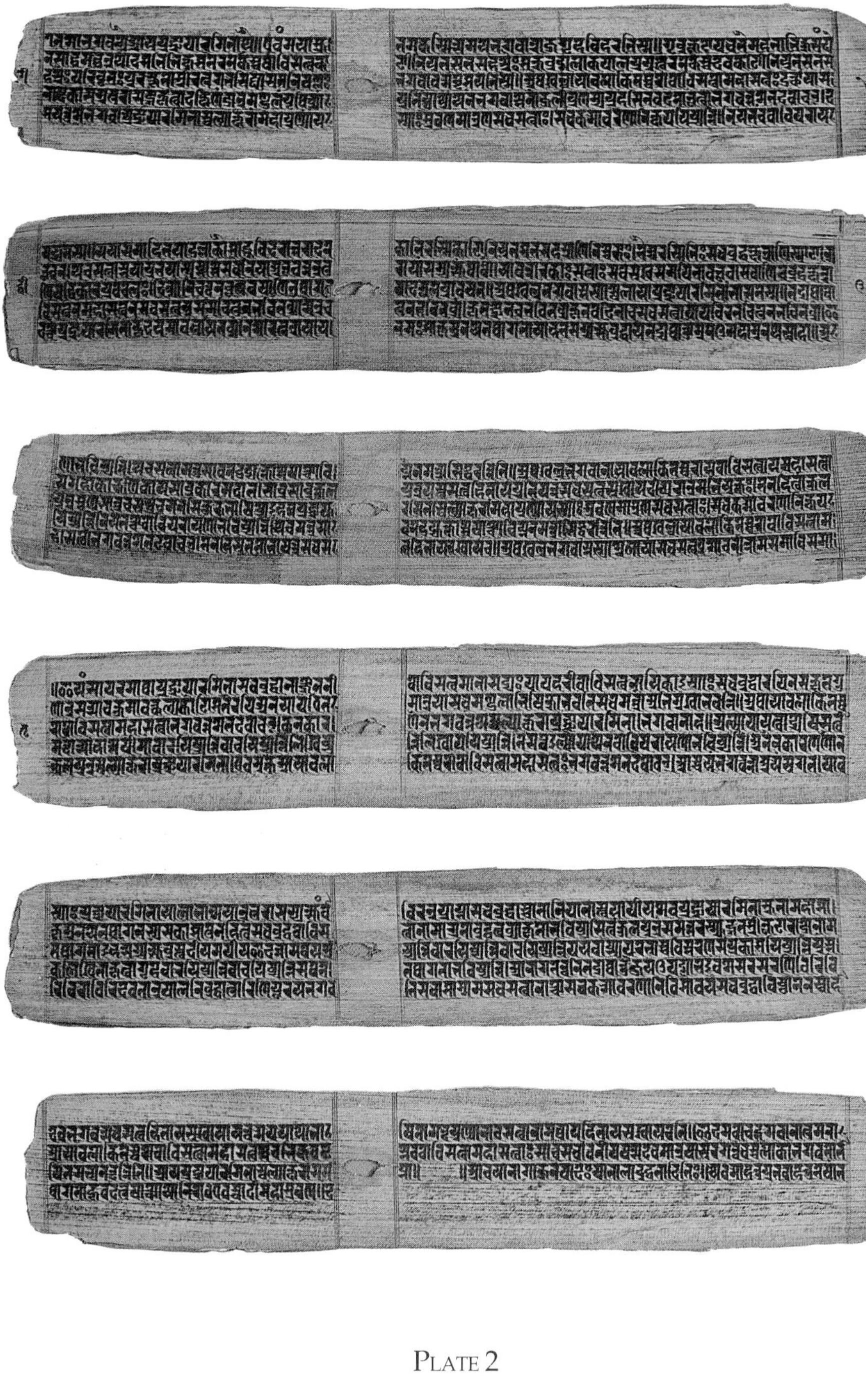

PLATE 2

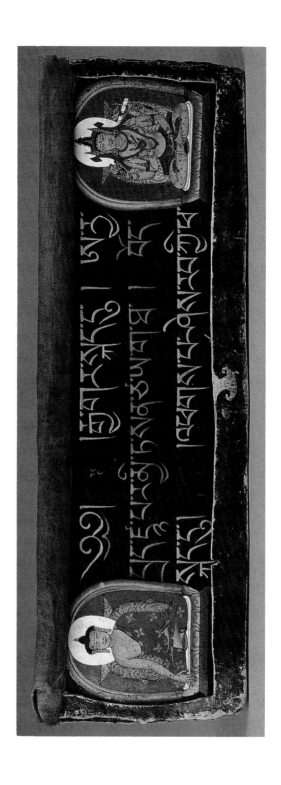

Plate 3

PLATE 4

I.

THE HEART SŪTRA

The Heart Sūtra was among the first of the Prajñāpāramitā teachings to be translated from the Sanskrit. It is considered to contain in its few lines the essence, or condensed meaning, of the entire Prajñāpāramitā. Our translation here is the eighth century work of the great translator Rinchen-De, under master Vimalamitra. Two other great translators, Gelo and Namkha, in collaboration with other Indian masters such as the Tibetan Vairocana, refined this version. Further refinement was undertaken to ensure that every word conveyed the correct meaning in Tibetan. In this way, Rinchen-De's version became the standard, immensely popular text which Tibetans have memorized, recited, and contemplated ever since.

THE TITLE

According to King Trisong Detsen's request, all the titles of the Prajñāpāramitā teachings were left in Sanskrit. Here, the title reads: *Bhagavatī Prajñāpāramitā Hṛdaya.*

Bhagavatī: *Bhaga* means "fortune." *Vatī* means "possessor" and is a feminine. Thus, one of the meanings of *bhagavatī* is literally "fortunate one." The Tibetans translated *bhagavatī* into three words: *Chom Den Dema (bCom-ldan-'das-ma). Chom* means "subdued, destroyed." *Den* means "to be in possession." *De* means "gone beyond, transcended." These are the conditions for achieving the state of buddhahood. *Ma* refers to the realizer, the wisdom itself, which has destroyed negative forces, taken possession of all good qualities of saṃsāra and nirvāṇa, and then gone beyond all extremes. What is destroyed? The negative, or demonic forces, also called *māras*, which are fourfold: 1) the demon of emotions; 2) the demon of aggregates; 3) the demon of death and dissolution; 4) the demon of distraction or of sensual indulgence. Once these powerful forces have receded, realization dawns, and one is said to be in possession of the six glories of both saṃsāra and nirvāṇa. These are: 1) dignity; 2) great fortune; 3) fame and renown; 4) power; 5) beauty; 6) health and longevity.

What is gone beyond, or transcended, are saṃsāra and nirvāṇa. All the great masters have realized that both nirvāṇa and saṃsāra are relative states of mind. Deluded sentient beings, however, always focus on extremes. In the exclusive logic of duality they insist that "if you go beyond saṃsāra, you must be in nirvāṇa," or "if you are not in nirvāṇa, you must be in saṃsāra." In the enlightened state of the absolute, saṃsāra and nirvāṇa are recognized as equal.

Bhagavatī, Chomdendema, is the one who has achieved enlightenment, or buddhahood. This term refers not to a physically existing person, but rather to the absolute state of Prajñāpāramitā itself, which has emerged from obscuration. *Bhagavatī* is considered as feminine because, through realization of her own nature, she gives birth to the buddhas of the three times, and thus is the mother of the so-called "Four Noble Children" on the path: shrāvaka-buddhas, pratyekabuddhas, bodhisattvas, and buddhas. Buddha Shākyamuni, teaching elsewhere in the Prajñāpāramitā, says that "those people who would become shrāvakas must learn to practice the Prajñāpāramitā; those who aspire to be a pratyekabuddha must learn and practice the Prajñāpāramitā; those who would achieve bodhisattva realization must learn and practice the Prajñāpāramitā;

and those who would accomplish buddhahood must learn and practice the Prajñāpāramitā."

Prajña translates into Tibetan as *sherab* (*shes-rab*)— "supreme wisdom." In Sanskrit *pra* means "supreme," or "highest," and *jña* is "knowledge" or "wisdom." It is supreme wisdom because what it knows or understands is the meaning of our true, absolute nature, and there is no meaning or knowledge higher than this.

Pāramitā means "beyond," or "the other shore." It also can be translated as "perfection" in some contexts. In Tibetan *pāramitā* is *paröltuchinpa* (*pha-rol-tu-phyin-pa*), "cross to the other shore." The other shore, the far shore, is the shore beyond extremes where supreme and perfect wisdom will awaken us.

Hṛdaya translates as *nyingpo* (*snying-po*) in Tibetan. In English it means "the heart," in this case signifying essence or core. This refers to two things. First, there are Prajñāpāramitā texts of differing lengths. The longest is 100,000 stanzas; there are others in 25,000 stanzas, 18,000, 8,000, 700, 500, and 300 stanzas respectively. *The Heart Sūtra*, however—the most condensed at only 25 stanzas—is the core of them all. Second, *hṛdaya* refers to the distilled, essential message of this teaching itself, called the "view." It is the view of supreme wisdom recognizing great emptiness, the pure essence. It is the view of Prajñāpāramitā. If we were to condense *The Heart Sūtra* down to an even more succinct message, it would be the single syllable Ah [Tib. *ah*].

Now, through hearing the explanation of the title, you have gained a general idea of what *The Heart Sūtra* is about.

MAIN TEXT

"Thus I Have Heard"

This line stands at the beginning of all the sūtras. It was placed there by command of Buddha Shākyamuni to the disciples he had entrusted with the task of collecting and editing his teachings before his paranirvāna.

In the Tibetan translation, these four words point to the five perfect conditions of the teaching. How these five perfections relate to "Thus I Have Heard" is as follows:

Thus—indicates the perfect teacher, Buddha Shākyamuni, who removed the veil of obscurations and pointed to the ultimate truth within.

I—refers to the perfect students, individuals gathered in the teacher's perfect retinue, the disciples who wrote this down.

Have Heard—The perfect teaching is what is heard.

In the Tibetan version, there are two more words:

Time (Tib. *dus*)—The perfect time is undisturbed by mind, emotions, or environment. Its peacefulness allows the power of the teaching to manifest.

Place (Tib. *na*)—difficult to translate in English, *na* indicates the perfect place through a meaning of sameness, or being together.

THE FIVE PERFECTIONS

Perfect Teacher: The 1,000 buddhas of the Fortunate Aeon are the perfect teachers; of them, Shākyamuni is the fourth. This aeon is called "Fortunate" because buddhas will manifest in it—a rare occurrence.

Perfect Students: The retinue of students consists of two types—ordinary and extraordinary. Of the ordinary, there are four kinds who were always present whenever Buddha Shākyamuni would teach. They are those who have taken vows: men and women, respectively, belonging to either the ordained or laity. These are called the four common, or ordinary, gatherings of Buddha Shākyamuni. Of the extraordinary, there were the great bodhisattvas, such as Chenrezi (Avalokiteshvara) and Mañjushrī, and the great arhats such as Shāriputra and Maudgalyāyana. Nonhuman beings too, gods and celestials, would participate. This whole gathering is referred to as the perfect students.

Perfect Teaching: The Prajñāpāramitā belongs to the second turning of the Dharma Wheel by Buddha Shākyamuni. In it he revealed the true nature of all phenomena in saṃsāra and nirvāṇa.

Perfect Time: According to Buddhist cosmology, our universe was created by the fleeting and fortuitous combination of otherwise disparate elements. Within its given lifetime of some twenty aeons, it will experience eighteen cycles of rising to a Golden Age and falling to a Degenerate Age. Currently we are living in a Degenerate Age of our Fortunate Æon, a time when—its label notwithstanding—spiritual energy is at a peak. Buddha Shākyamuni made his appearance at the beginning of this Degenerate Age. Thus, for those who wish to practice and to understand the meaning of Prajñāpāramitā, it is the perfect time.

Perfect Place: Vulture Peak, where Lord Buddha turned the wheel of the Mahāyāna, is according to Buddhism the geographic center of the world, and not far from the spot where he reached enlightenment. The special wisdom energy of this perfect place allows realization to grow.

These are the Five Perfections.

> "Once the Blessed One was dwelling in Rājagṛha
> at Vulture Peak Mountain, together with a great gathering
> of the sangha of monks and the sangha of bodhisattvas.
> At that time the Blessed One entered the samādhi that
> examines the dharmas called 'profound illumination.'"

When Lord Buddha entered the clear, profound state of samādhi, he appeared from the outside to be simply meditating. His students, however, were aware that in his enlightenment state he was emanating streams of brilliant light from his crown, forehead, throat, heart and naval chakras, as well as from every pore of his golden body.

The Buddha's "samādhi which examines the dharmas" is the samādhi that recognizes the true, ultimate nature of every phenomenon, in both saṃsāra and nirvāṇa, externally and internally. This true nature is the *mahāshūnyatā*, the great emptiness, the profound meaning beyond words, speech and mental conceptualization. Within this clear, profound samādhi, Lord Buddha was also able to secure the ultimate benefit of others. The beams of pure light pouring forth from his body to every direction and realm, then returning to be reabsorbed, then radiating out again, were pacifying the sufferings and removing the obscurations of all sentient beings.

At the ultimate level of realization of the true nature, we do not just blend into everything and become inactive. In fact, at that level we become actively beneficial, and such realization makes it possible for us to reach millions of sentient beings and dissolve the obstacles to their liberation. That is the profound illumination.

> "At the same time noble Avalokiteshvara,
> the bodhisattva mahāsattva, contemplating the profound
> practice of the Prajñāpāramitā, saw the five skandhas
> to be empty in nature."

I will speak later about the five skandhas, and their natural emptiness. First, I would like to explain who the bodhisattva and the arhat are, and why a discussion between them is considered a teaching of the Buddha.

Bodhisattva, a Sanskrit word, is *chang chub sempa (byang-chub-sems-dpa')* in Tibetan. *Bodhi* means "enlightened, awakened," freed from the obscurations of dualistic and conceptual thinking. The nature of *bodhi* is primordial wisdom. *Sattva* means "courageous being." The enlightened being, the bodhisattva, must be courageous because he no longer exists merely for himself and his family and friends. He has dedicated the activities of this body, speech and mind to bringing joy and happiness to all sentient beings—not just ten or a hundred, a few thousand or a hundred thousand, but to sentient beings as limitless in number as space itself. According to the Buddha, the bodhisattva's courage has to be equally infinite in scope, making neither exceptions nor discriminations.

The duration of this courage too, must be infinite, if you are to work for all of them. It must continue on for hundreds and hundreds of aeons, equal to the infinity of sentient beings who are suffering. Courage must, too, remain changeless and indestructible as a mountain. Like the earth, which remains earth regardless of what is built upon it, or a bridge which remains a bridge regardless of the people or cars that traffic upon it, the bodhisattva must help others with perfect and pure intensity. There will inevitably be some who do not recognize what you are doing; they might be mean or stubborn towards you. Never be bored or upset, just continuously radiate courage until sentient beings are free from suffering. Then you will be known as a bodhisattva.

Avalokiteshvara is actually more than a being who has become enlightened—he has also achieved the state of buddhahood. Therefore in this teaching he is referred to as the twice courageous one—in Sanskrit, *bodhisattva-mahāsattva,* or "greatly courageous being." He exists on two levels: on the relative level, in order to help sentient beings, he appears as a bodhisattva; but on the absolute level, because he is totally enlightened, he is indistinguishable from the Buddha's infinite compassion.

In Tibet Avalokiteshvara is called Chenrezi (*spyan-ras-gzigs*), and his practice is very popular. Using the skillful means of an enlightened being, Avalokiteshvara returned to saṃsāra as a student of the Buddha Shākyamuni in order to reveal the meaning of the absolute teaching. His image appears frequently in thangkas, and may take many different forms, with two, four, or sometimes a thousand arms.

Arhat is a Sanskrit word meaning "he who subdues or destroys enemies." This does not refer to an external, physically existent enemy, but rather is a metaphor referring to the inner enemies of ego-clinging, the emotions, and their concomitant obscurations. An arhat has completely uprooted these enemies. The arhat Shāriputra was one of Buddha Shākyamuni's two foremost disciples. Of the hundreds of disciples of the Buddha, Shāriputra and Maudgalyāyana were considered supreme—the supreme disciples of Buddha Shākyamuni. In thangkas they are often depicted as the two student-attendants, Shāriputra to the right, Maudgalyāyana to the left, standing beside the Buddha. Not only do these two symbolize all the disciples of the Buddha, but Shāriputra and Maudgalyāyana also represent two attributes of the arhat: supreme knowledge or wisdom on the one hand, and supreme siddhi or miraculous power on the other. Shāriputra's wisdom and Maudgalyāyana's power were considered a challenge or standard of accomplishment to all of the arhats.

Perhaps you are wondering why this discussion between

Avalokiteshvara and Shāriputra is considered a teaching of Buddha Shākyamuni. There are many different levels on which a buddha can give teachings. Although sometimes he can talk directly as ordinary teachers do, he does not necessarily have to do so. There are times when he need use only bodily gestures. This particular teaching was transmitted originally from mind to mind, by the power of Buddha Shākyamuni's meditative concentration. Such teachings, of which *The Heart Sūtra* is one of the best known, are said to be "blessed" or "buddha-influenced"—influenced by the enlightened wisdom power alone. Thus it is said that the wisdom power of Lord Buddha's meditation, the Prajñāpāramitā, became manifest in the words spoken by Avalokiteshvara and Shāriputra.

THE FIVE SKANDHAS

> **"O Shāriputra, a son or daughter of noble qualities who
> wishes to practice the profound Prajñāpāramitā should
> regard things in the following way. The five skandhas
> should be seen to be completely empty in nature."**

It is important to understand what the skandhas are, and exactly how they are empty. This is one of *The Heart Sūtra*'s main points. Explanation in detail of this subject is contained in what is called the Abhidharma section, or third basket, of Buddha Shākyamuni's Tripiṭaka, the three baskets of teachings which explicate the general system of Buddhism. The Vajrayāna, taught mostly after Lord Buddha's paranirvāṇa, is either included in the third basket as part of the Abhidharma, or simply called the fourth basket. The Vajrayāna, Vinaya, Sūtra, and Abhidharma, together constitute the complete teachings of Buddha Shākyamuni.

The wisdom of the Abhidharma knows the phenomenal world through a clear understanding of the two truths, relative and absolute. Because we are seeking to perceive both the

skandhas and their emptiness, we must be able to see and understand clearly whatever arises exactly as it is, without exaggerating
or depreciating it, adding to it or subtracting from it. Emptiness is
not made or created by anybody; it is natural, unborn, naturally
uncreated, and uncompounded.

According to Abhidharma, whatever exists in this phenomenal world, saṃsāra or nirvāṇa, can be condensed into two groups:
compounded things and uncompounded things. Nothing whatsoever falls outside these two categories. The five skandhas belong to
the category of compounded things, and in fact include them all.
Skandha, in Sanskrit, means "heap": many things piled together,
like a big flea market or yard sale, not just a single, indivisible
thing. In English we call the five skandhas the five "aggregates."
The five skandhas are: 1) form; 2) feeling; 3) conception; 4) mental
formations; 5) consciousness.

1) Form

Form has dimension and weight. Form has the power to block, or
impede. When we say form, we are not just referring to our bodies,
but to everything that has mass and offers resistance. Everything
material is part of the form aggregate.

To clarify this further, the Abhidharma divides the form
skandha into fifteen subdivisions: four causal forms and eleven
resultant forms. The four causal forms are the elements earth,
water, fire, air. Space is not counted separately as it is everywhere,
causes no resistance, and has no mass or material structure. It is
through these four elements that ten of the eleven resultant forms
have their cause, their origin and their molecular development in
the material world. These ten resultant forms are further divided
into five results appearing as the subject and five results appearing
as the object. The former are the eye, ear, nose, tongue, and body
organs; the latter are light, sound, smell, taste and touch.

There is one more resultant form which comes to exist neither as an element nor as a consciousness. It is called "invisible form," and is an energy, power or ability of the individual that is very special. It can exert a strong influence to guide you in daily life if you have the confidence in yourself or in your ideas to be aware of it. Invisible form exists purely at the mental-conceptual level. It can harm you as well as help you.[2]

That is the explanation of the form skandha, comprising the roots of all visible phenomena. But there is a deeper level of understanding form and how it appears to us. The most immediate basis of the form skandha is manifest at a gross level, but this in turn arises on the basis of a much more subtle level which some Buddhists, for lack of a better term at that time, called "partless atoms." Here, millions of sub-atomic particles, themselves insubstantial, come together or aggregate and give the appearance of mass. Thus, there is nothing solid on which everything rests and no final, independently existing form. Through infinite combinations of infinite "partless atoms," an interdependent, caused and conditioned display arises in the form of the four causal and eleven resultant objects. This is the heap, the aggregate, the skandha, of form.

2) Feeling

Feeling is the second skandha. Again, feeling refers to many things aggregated together, but whereas form is mass, feeling is considered to be part of the mind. Mass and consciousness are quite different. Because as ordinary beings we have no clear understanding about the aggregates, we may think that feelings—or emotions—are identical with our bodies. Of course they have a very strong connection, but in their function they are quite different.

Feeling is important because it conditions our mental aggregate and determines what, in the end, we experience. It is catego-

---

[2] Examples of invisible forms are vows, decisions, names, labels, positions and titles.

rized into eighteen types based on each of the six senses, in one of three feeling states: attraction, aversion, or indifference. Many causes come together to create a particular feeling. We like to have happy, pleasurable feelings, and we reject feelings of sadness. Our attachment to pleasurable states is so strong that when conditions thwart us, we become angry, frustrated, or jealous. Many differing karmas result, which then become causes for future visions and experiences. Feeling is therefore one of the most important influences affecting our life in saṃsāra.

3) Conception

The third skandha is the function of analysis and investigation. The multitude of impulses that make up the "heap" of conception can be understood as the tendency to create distinctions and cling to them within a dualistic framework. This conception of duality causes further attachment. Size, color, purity, location, sex and species all arise as concepts within the third aggregate called conception. All this happens primarily beneath the conscious level. The mind follows unconscious, habitual patterns, assigning names to experiences, and in this way fabricates a world of mental objects which cannot be said to have any substantial existence outside the stream of mind.

Some conceptions are born with us, and others we have simply added. For instance, all rules, systems, and traditions practiced in our country, village, or family are mental creations—ideas—and thus part of the conception aggregate. All things we have learned and are learning are conceptions. What is permitted and what is forbidden are conceptions. There is nothing which we can say exists as an objective reality.

We can verify this simply by examining and observing it ourselves. We live according to judgments which solidify and add certainty to our otherwise nameless and shifting world. For example, when you were a child looking at a picture of a cow, you were told to say "cow" by a parent or teacher until you learned it. If you did not learn it, they would let you know you had failed or were not doing well. The word must be associated with the picture and the two mingled, until you can say "cow." We must work at this because the picture of the cow and the word "cow" have no intrinsic relationship. They are two totally different things. The naming process results in a mere concept, or idea, which we then grasp as if it were a concrete reality.

In different countries the same cow has many different names. These reflect the different ways of thinking—all concepts. When Tibetans see that picture they are not going to say "cow." They will say "ba." In India they will say "gais." One says cow, one says ba, and one says gais. Who is really correct? Who is wrong? Even if they go to the Supreme Court for a decision, who can really say one is true and the other is false? I think either everyone is right or everyone is wrong.

Like this simple example, everything is built upon concepts and judgments, not on objectively, independently existing realities. Notions of cleanliness and beauty change from one culture to another. In Tibet alone, the traditions and beliefs of the people in the east and west are quite opposite. But these examples are rather obvious. They are systems based upon dualistic ideas, like two different gloves, back and front, or east and west. This universe has many such arbitrary systems, more profound and varied than these. They are all part of the labeling, clinging, idea-creating skandha of conception.

4)   Mental Formations

The term "formation" is used for the fourth skandha to convey a sense of bringing into being, in the realm of mind as well as body. This is the aggregate of karma, which starts in the mind and is reflected in the speech and the body. Whatever action is performed in this world is part of the fourth skandha.

The Buddhist term karma is a Sanskrit word meaning "action," or "activity." Buddha Shākyamuni taught that all karma arises from mind. Mental states are the producers and creators, while body and speech are their agents. The mind's action flows through the channels of body and speech, becomes visible outwardly by reflection, and returns back again as karma rotates.

We can understand karma mostly through inference only. It creates things which, though not inherently existent, arise nevertheless. Then, in a continuous reproductive cycle, these things change and become in turn the causes of more things. In the physical world, for example, if we see a flower, we infer the causes and conditions which brought it into visible being. Though these causes and conditions may not be obviously present, we can make inferences about them, about the flower's past. We can also predict the future without being mistaken. If we see a flower seed, we can safely say that if this is a good seed, which is the cause, and it has the right conditions with which to mingle, there will definitely be a result, the flower. The flower is inevitable, whether you want it or not; the causes and conditions transcend our preferences.

This pattern works the same way on the inner phenomena of our mental stream. Activity of speech and body occur on a gross level which is felt, seen or heard by others. Mental activity is more subtle and profound. It operates continuously in everyone. With concentration we can locate and observe it in ourselves, but we cannot see another's very clearly. We may feel it but not be able to see or perceive it directly. Through inference we can determine the mental activity of another person the same way we infer fire from smoke. All this activity is part of the skandha of mental formations.

5) Consciousness

The fifth skandha is very powerful. The functions of the skandhas of conception and mental formations arise from it. It is based upon a very subtle state known as the *ālaya* in Sanskrit, the *kunzhi* (*kun-*

gzhi) in Tibetan, or "subconscious storehouse" in English. This is a subtle consciousness, neither positive nor negative, that is barely moving. All our information and habit patterns are collected here and stored. They arise again and are reflected in experience according to the presence of causes and conditions. The consciousness skandha is not dependent upon the five organs of sense, although when these organs are activated, consciousness functions according to each one, whether eye, ear, nose, tongue, or body consciousness. This is as if a single light were shining through five different windows. Sense objects entering these windows are gathered in the consciousness, which then judges them as good, bad, or neutral.

Without these five consciousness organs, the mental consciousness can still experience things. When we go to sleep, for example, and the five sense organs are inactive, the mind continues working in the dream state, playing itself back to itself within its own subject-object universe. The many habit patterns of its past arise, and sometimes it even experiences the future. Consciousness is quick and powerful, faster than you can imagine. It can control our experience of the three times and also it can change things.

Consciousness itself is based upon a momentary state. Hundreds of millions of moments, instants of continual change, are moving through past, present and future. It is not a single thing stretching all the way back from the beginning until now, forever unchanging. It is not a solid object. It is more like a current or continuity such as a river, composed of these billions of flowing instants.

Consciousness can be either positive and virtuous or negative and non-virtuous. Qualities such as loving-kindness, compassion, devotion and clear understanding of the true nature are all considered aspects of positive consciousness. If mind is manifesting qualities such as anger, jealousy, attachment and ignorance, it is considered negative and non-virtuous. This is the consciousness skandha.

To summarize, the five skandhas of form, feeling, conception, mental formations and consciousness are compounded and inter-dependent things. No skandha is solid or single, but is rather a flux of many hundreds of things in combination. We never exist for one moment outside of these five aggregates. They are the foundation of saṃsāra, the enablers of our clinging and attachment. They are also, however, the key to our enlightenment, for it is only by our understanding them, by our gaining a clear picture of what they are and how they function, that nirvāṇa can become present in our mind-stream. When this occurs, noble Avalokiteshvara's answer to Shāriputra that the five skandhas are empty in nature will become clear.

EMPTINESS

The reason Avalokiteshvara uses the term "nature" in con-junction with emptiness is very important. This emptiness is not fabricated by anybody—not even by a buddha. It is already there naturally, a natural condition or basis of all phenomena and all five skandhas. The emptiness of the aggregates is unfabricated and natural the same way the heat of fire or the wetness of water is unfabricated. It is simply the nature of all phenomena to be empty. Avalokiteshvara gives Shāriputra a more detailed explanation through use of the following four axioms.

> **"Form is emptiness. Emptiness is form. Form is none other than emptiness. Emptiness is none other than form."**

1) **"Form is emptiness."** If we try to disassemble a form down to its minutest atoms, we will lose the form, it will not be identifiable as the form it was when we began. We can subdivide even further into subatomic particles, or "partless atoms," as they are called in Buddhist philosophical terminology, and the form is changed again.

For example, you see this watch. Everybody sees this watch. If we break it up into smaller parts, its identity as a solid, independently existing thing disappears. We cannot find any single watch among these parts anymore. So it is with all phenomena. We see and feel that they exist until we begin to investigate and analyze with our certainty-wisdom (Tib. *nge shes*, see p. 60, 68, 94). What is the nature of these phenomena? They can all be destructured and disassembled into a subatomic state which indeterminately commingles with great emptiness. The ultimate, empty ground state of all these infinitesimal "seeming-particles" is the basic reality of the phenomenal world.

But it is not as if form and emptiness are two independently existing things such as right and left. Avalokiteshvara stressed to Shāriputra that form *is* emptiness, rather than asserting that form is *like* emptiness, or form *becomes* emptiness, or *used to be* emptiness. He did this so that students would avoid the mistake of nihilism and eternalism, that is, the making of either form or emptiness into some kind of dualistic absolute. If we are liberated from clinging to forms, then we can experience them as merely appearing rather than as solidly existing. Appearance is empty from the beginning.

2) **"Emptiness is form."** Avalokiteshvara clarifies this idea further with his second statement, the reverse of the first one. Emptiness cannot be separated from form any more than form can be separated from emptiness. Just as the nature of form is emptiness, the nature of emptiness is to have form. Emptiness is not a state of nothingness, or black hole, as put forth by the nihilistic view. Rather, emptiness and form co-exist in the same state. You could say that emptiness is a fullness of form which is reflected within interdependent arising. Knowing that this is so liberates us from attachment to the non-existence of the phenomenal world, including the non-existence of death and time.

3) **"Form is none other than emptiness."** At this point, you might be thinking still that there are two different things, form and

emptiness, which exist in a unified state: both existence and non-existence forged together somehow. In the third statement, Avalokiteshvara intends to free us from that concept, for it is not the ultimate level of truth, but still a level of clinging and fixation to the idea that there are two different, independent entities which are joined. The solidity of form and the nothingness of emptiness are only apparent, and therefore it cannot be that a concrete existence and an absolute non-existence are in some way melded together. In the state free from all extreme concepts, emptiness and form, from primordial time, have always existed intimately as one.

4) **"Emptiness is none other than form."** We have reached the level of understanding that the ideas themselves of existence and non-existence are faulty and extreme. However, in his final statement, Avalokiteshvara wants us to know that we still have not transcended clinging, for the idea that existence and non-existence do not exist is still an extreme position. The argument subverts our ability to hold onto any position whatsoever. We are cut loose from the cycle of dualistic concepts to rest in the great equanimity, the state of simplicity, the great completion.

To summarize: Axiom 1 cuts attachment to things as solidly existing; Axiom 2 cuts attachment to things as solidly not existing; Axiom 3 cuts attachment to both existence and non-existence as existing together; Axiom 4 cuts attachment to the idea of neither existence nor non-existence as existing. These four statements cover the range of any idea a sentient being could possibly have. Things must either exist or not exist; or perhaps they somehow are both existent and non-existent together; or finally, perhaps they are in a state of neither existing nor not-existing.

In Buddhism, the true nature is beyond words, beyond limits of our imagination. Otherwise we would be able to define it with our ordinary mind, by means of one of these four statements. Thus Avalokiteshvara expressed the ultimate nature of the form aggregate as something inexpressible.

**"In this same way feeling, conception, mental formations,
and consciousness are empty."**

Now we bring the remaining four skandhas into focus by means of the same technique, the four axioms. Avalokiteshvara does not spell out the argument for each one as he did with form. We ourselves can do this as follows:

Feeling is emptiness; emptiness is feeling; feeling is none other than emptiness; emptiness is none other than feeling.

Conception is emptiness; emptiness is conception; conception is none other than emptiness; emptiness is none other than conception.

Mental formations are emptiness; emptiness is mental formations; mental formations are none other than emptiness; emptiness is none other than mental formations.

Consciousness is emptiness; emptiness is consciousness; consciousness is none other than emptiness; emptiness is none other than consciousness.

All five aggregates are identical with and inseparable from emptiness.

THE TWO TRUTHS

To further clarify the way the skandhas and their emptiness are connected, it is helpful to analyze and examine our experiences and perceptions according to the theory of the two truths: relative and absolute. In general, the mundane mind understands the two truths as two separate things. We do not usually consider the objects of our senses—what we see, hear, taste, smell, and touch—to be intimately connected to our consciousness. The everyday world is something we consider to be absolutely, independently existing, yet its tenuousness and relativity remain completely hidden from us.

In order to arrive at an appreciation of the absolute emptiness basis of all phenomena, it is necessary to unravel the fabric of this misconception by means of our certainty wisdom. Taking what we have learned about the skandhas, we see that form, or physical mass, dominates the superficial level of our world. Although everything seems to be material, and it even seems that such materiality is the basic and all-pervading principle, gradually we come to realize that the greater percentage of our experience has its source deep within the subtle, invisible, immaterial realm.

This realm is where the last four of the five skandhas manifest. They are purely mental phenomena, from which the first skandha of form arises. It doesn't take a lot of logic to comprehend the primacy of mind over matter. Wherever and whenever mind decides to go, the body naturally follows. If mind decides to stay, so too will you. When mind is appreciative or when it is critical, speech, too, will be appreciative or critical. Sometimes, however, it does take a lot of analysis for us to face that it is we ourselves who control whether we are happy or unhappy, not other people or external things. The only time our bodies do not follow our minds is at the moment of death, when they will sink back into the elements right here on earth while our consciousness travels onward to the next life.

Having established that mind always has, is, and will be the highest principle, it is important to continually challenge our mundane perceptions. If we examine in detail the aggregate of feeling, for example, is it not just as insubstantial and transitory as is form? Once the fires of attachment and hatred have subsided, or the false security of indifference has been shattered, it is easy to see that the power of such emotions becomes present through the illusion of some kind of solid reality the emotions do not in fact possess. Each skandha succumbs in this way to analysis, until we arrive at the place where every one of our experiences has its starting point: the fifth, most important skandha of consciousness.

It is here that the act of grasping is most difficult to release, despite the subtlety of the level on which it operates. It is nothing less than the root of saṃsāra: the dualistic functioning of consciousness controlling every aspect of phenomena through the skandhas. These subtle, deluded thoughts, too, are not solid or fixed entities. It is important to realize that all grasping is the work of fleeting, relative, mental states, and that freedom from all grasping is the absolute, natural state. This mind, according to Avalokiteshvara, is also emptiness. It seems to exist on a relative level, yet if someone asks you "show me your mind," what can you show them? On the absolute level, all our thoughts are like clouds, and the consciousness skandha cannot be found anywhere. By clearly understanding the emptiness nature of consciousness, experience and realization will come.

"Thus, Shāriputra, are all dharmas emptiness. They have no characteristics. They are unborn and unceasing;"

Avalokiteshvara now begins to specify the empty ways that all phenomena exist. Whether objective, subjective, outer or inner, all dharmas are definable from the relative point of view as having certain characteristics. Because they seem to exist in time, coming into and going out of being, we say they have a previous cause for such being, something which generates, develops, and gives birth to those sets of qualities. Furthermore, phenomena quit their present mode of being. They are themselves the seed for something else to happen, or future results.

From the absolute point of view, these three factors of characteristics, birth, and cessation cannot be found. Their three emptinesses are called the Three Doors to Liberation: 1) no characteristics; 2) no birth; 3) no cessation. This is also expressed as: 1) signlessness (no cause); 2) wishlessness (no expectation of result); and 3) emptiness nature (of both).

1) **No characteristics.** To illustrate what we mean by characteristics, we can use the following examples. Some characteristics of the sun are light and heat; some characteristics of water are moisture and fluidity; some characteristics of flowers are a stalk, petals, pistils, color and beauty. Some characteristics of animals are four feet and a mouth. Human characteristics are standing on two legs, having no tail, no horns, and having many many thoughts restlessly arising and producing one thing after the other. We can see that each individual entity has its own characteristics on the relative level.

On the absolute level we say that these same aggregates have no characteristics because, under investigation, they break down just as we have already discussed. There are no identifying qualities which are permanent, unchanging, or fixed. The nature of all characteristics is emptiness.

2) **No birth.** On the level of the relative truth, everything we see has a cause. A cause is the agent of generation and development, or birth and growth. However, no matter how hard we try, we will be unable to pinpoint and isolate the exact moment a phenomenon comes into being. Instead, we will find insubstantial flux. Though relatively speaking we find causes and effects, strict analysis will lead us to the absolute nature. For example, a phenomenon can only have a definite birth if it is a definite result. What is the relationship or connection between cause and effect? Either the result already exists simultaneously with the cause or it does not, or neither of these is true, or both are true. By analyzing relative phenomena this way we arrive at the absolute, empty nature of all that merely appears to have a moment of coming into being. The absolute is known as the unborn, because it is uncaused and uncompounded.

3) **No cessation.** Cessation happens only as the result of birth. If there has been no birth, there can be no death. Emptiness, the absolute truth of phenomena existing in time, is often described as

being like the son of a barren woman: he has never been born, has never developed, and has no notion whatsoever of death. Such is the reality of the absolute nature of all phenomena, subjective or objective. The three doors to liberation are the three great emptinesses of the primordial nature.

"... neither impure nor free from impurity; ..."

In Sanskrit this is expressed as *sarva dharma svabhāva shuddho 'ham,* which you might know from your Vajrayāna practice. It means "all phenomena are totally pure from the beginning." According to our relative perception, our world is filled with errors, faults, stains and obscurations. We feel quite righteous about this. The faults of others, the imperfections of our environment, sometimes seem to be even more solid than tables and chairs. Our own flaws as well, if we are aware of them at all, sometimes can seem insurmountable or unforgiveable. But these, too, dissolve under close inspection and analysis. We cannot say that impurities exist anywhere, so how can we say we must become free of them? The idea of purity depends upon the idea of impurity. Total purity from the beginning transcends such dualistic notions.

"They neither decrease nor increase."

Because the absolute nature of reality is unchanging and incorruptible, it cannot be decreased or increased: it is unquantifiable. When we rest in the absolute nature, we are not expanding it in any way; when we begin to wander away from it, we are not shrinking it. The enlightened ones understood that absolute reality doesn't change under any circumstances, whether beings recognize it or not. Even Lord Buddha did not change the absolute nature in any way when he turned the Wheel of the Dharma.

In the more elaborated Prajñāpāramitā teachings, it is often stated that this absolute nature, also known as buddha nature, is the inheritance of each and every sentient being. All of us, regardless of intelligence, character, or species, possess the buddha nature, and it is the buddha nature we seek to discover when we seek enlightenment. I say "discover" because it is not something essentially different from ourselves; we need not fabricate it or construct it on top of something else. When our buddha nature is revealed, we gain access to its many attributes, such as wisdom, compassion and loving-kindness. These qualities are extremely valuable. They guide us in times of delusion, and they radiate out to others in the form of communication, friendship, joy, and happiness. When relaxed and cheerful, sentient beings can actually share and work together.

If this absolute nature cannot be affected by increase or decrease, and all sentient beings possess it already, then why do we need to practice? It is often said that the buddha nature exists only as a potential, or spark, in the ordinary being; its brilliance is obscured by many layers of dualistic concepts, the bad mental habits of infinite lifetimes. Therefore it has always been necessary that we be clearly instructed in the truth of our relative existence. The many methods taught by the Buddha have the power to peel away our obscurations and allow us to see the truth for ourselves. Although these methods are many and varied, they all have as their essence the twofold mind-training of compassion and wisdom. Compassion and loving-kindness in themselves are undisputed as the greatest treasure of all sentient beings; even animals and insects are able to recognize their value. Compassion with the wisdom of emptiness together constitute the essential practices on the path to enlightenment—they are the great ornaments of the bodhisattva.

GROUND, PATH, AND FRUIT

**"Therefore, Shāriputra, emptiness has no form, no feeling,
no conception, no mental formations, no consciousness ..."**

To summarize and further illustrate the teaching on emptiness,
Avalokiteshvara proceeds to list the factors of the ground, path,
and fruit as categorized in Buddhist doctrine.

The basic ground state of saṃsāra and nirvāṇa is divided into
the five aggregates, which have already been discussed, the subcat-
egories of the consciousness aggregate, and the twelve links of
interdependent causation.

In order to achieve the fruit of seeing this ground state as it is,
we must enter the path and apply the practices we have been
taught. The path, which has five stages, cannot be successfully
traversed unless the practitioner gains first a clear understanding
of saṃsāra's defects. This process is condensed in the core doctrine
of the Four Noble Truths: 1) the truth of suffering; 2) the cause of
suffering; 3) the truth of cessation; 4) the cause of cessation.

Finally, Avalokiteshvara speaks of the fruit, or attainment,
which is enlightenment. There is not one of these things which is
not based in emptiness. Now I will explain these in detail. We have
already discussed the five aggregates, so we will begin with the
next series, the twelve āyatanas, or sense-fields.

The Ground of Saṃsāra

**"... no eye, no ear, no nose, no tongue, no body, no mind; no
matter, no sound, no smell, no taste, no touch, no dharmas ..."**

The twelve *āyatanas*, or "sense-fields," all belong to the aggregate
of consciousness. Six are related to the subject and six are related to
the object. Of the subject, we have the consciousness of the eye, ear,
nose, tongue, body, mind; of the object, we have form, sound,
smell, taste, touch, and "dharmas," or in this case, mental objects.

"Dharmas" has at least ten different meanings, but here it is meant only in the sense of mental objects.

Āyatana is *kye che* (*skyed-mched*) in Tibetan. *Kye* means "to take birth," and *che* means "to spark, erupt." This is because the six different consciousnesses of the subject are completely latent, or inactive, unless sparked through contact with their corresponding six objects. This essential teaching of the Abhidharma is very important. If you can understand clearly the relationship between subject and object, or how consciousness depends upon contact with its objects, then you are no longer ignorant and confused about the relationship between the external and the internal.

> **"... no eye elements ... no mind elements,**
> **and no mind consciousness elements; ..."**

The Sanskrit *dhātu* is called *kham* (*khams*) in Tibetan. This means "element, seed"—something very fundamental which has potency and potential. These elements are a subdivision of the twelve sense-fields. They describe the participating factors in perception: subject and object, and in between, which form three sections of six each. The three sections are labelled the outer elements, inner elements, and secret elements, and their respective six subdivisions all correspond to the six different senses.

The six "outer" elements relating to external things correspond to the six object āyatanas of form, sound, smell, taste, touch, and mind.

The six "inner" elements are related to the eye, ear, nose, tongue, body, and mind organs. They are composed of both mind and matter, and therefore are positioned between the subject (secret) and the object (outer) elements.

It is important to note that the sense organ itself is different from the sense consciousness. If we don't look closely, the two are easily mistaken for one another, or even seem to be the same. However, the organ merely supports its corresponding consciousness. For example, when we say "the eye sees," we are not being entirely correct. It is our eye consciousness, not the organ, which is doing the seeing. If we were to sleep with our eyes open, as some people do, our eyes still will not see what is in front of us because our eye consciousness is inactive.

These sense consciousnesses all belong to the secret category of elements, and they are a function solely of the mental organ, the brain. The brain must receive its energy from the other five organs before it can construct mundane awareness. Within one subtle instant its six facets are able to transform that sense energy into information. Thus, the inner elements allow the secret elements to become active. By having an eye, ear, nose, tongue or body organ, the respective consciousnesses become active, and by having a mental organ, or brain, mental consciousness is established.

> **"... no ignorance, no end of ignorance ... no old age and**
> **death, no end of old age and death ..."**

This passage refers to the twelve *nidānas*, or links in the chain of causation. In Tibetan they are called *tendrel* (*rten-'brel*). They are the following: 1) ignorance; 2) karmic formations; 3) consciousness; 4) name and form; 5) the six senses; 6) contact; 7) feeling; 8) thirst; 9) clinging; 10) becoming; 11) birth; 12) old age and death.

This chain describes the sequence by which all the aggregates, sense-fields, and elements interact to keep sentient beings bound in a cycle of suffering. There is a very well-known Tibetan scroll painting which illustrates this, called the "Wheel of Life." In it, we see the Wrathful Lord of Impermanence holding in his mouth a large wheel divided into several concentric circles. Innermost are the symbols of the three root poisons: pig—ignorance; cock—attachment; and snake—hatred. Each is linked to the other, tail-to-mouth, to form a circle, illustrating the merry-go-round of the deluded mind. Ignorant of its empty nature, the mind clings to existence as a concrete reality. Under the spell of this solidity it then hates, and kills. The cycle begins anew as the mind continues to hide itself from the truth of its actions.

Moving outward in the wheel, we see sentient beings in their respective realms of birth, and at the rim, we see the sections of the twelve links of causation, "from ignorance up to old age and death." Everything begins with ignorance, and everything can end with clear wisdom, or a true understanding of the relative and absolute nature. To illustrate, if the cycle of suffering is like a fan, then ignorance is like the electricity. All we have to do is shut off the electricity and the fan will stop. If we replace the first link, ignorance, with wisdom, then all the ensuing links will dissolve one by one. We do not have to work on them separately.

Again, it is the emptiness of this system which Avalokiteshvara is stressing. The twelve interdependent links exist solely on the illusory level of relative truth; from the absolute level of truth, these links are rooted in emptiness, in primordial timelessness. Even the notion of old age and death is non-existent. By not realizing the nature of these twelve nidānas, we have a cyclical waxing and waning of emotional, physical and psychological problems. When the treadmill of saṃsāra has been shut down, and we are free of ignorance, we have attained the state of nirvāṇa, or enlightenment.

* * * * *

We have now completed the explanation of the five aggregates, twelve sense-fields, eighteen elements, and twelve links of causation, which together make up the illusory world of saṃsāra. They are the causes and conditions for saṃsāra's ceaseless rotation and for the endless spiral of births and deaths we must experience. Only by applying the powerful antidote of the absolute truth can we gain control over this elaborate compulsion. Investigating and analyzing, using the most sophisticated inner certainty wisdom like a microscope to observe external and internal things down to the particles, we find nothing. However, it is wrong to say that saṃsāra does not exist at all. In discovering emptiness, we find ourselves at the same time seeing the full display of saṃsāra in all its detail. This relative level at which saṃsāra can be said to exist is just as important to understand as the absolute level. Having cleared away our confusion and discovered the illusory nature of all reality, we do not cling, and all phenomena are liberated in primordial wisdom.

This concludes the discussion of the ground state of saṃsāra

The Path and Fruit

Avalokiteshvara continues with the Four Noble Truths, which motivate us to travel the paths to enlightenment.

> **"Likewise, there is no suffering, no origin of suffering,**
> **no cessation of suffering, no path; ..."**

1) **The Truth of Suffering**. The First Noble Truth is called *dug ngal* (*sdug-bsngal*) in Tibetan. To practice the path, we must have a clear understanding of the suffering that, as impermanence, pervades all existence. It is said that to the ordinary person, this impermanence is imperceptible as a hair on the palm of the hand, but to the enlightened ones, it feels as sharp as a hair in the eyeball. Though we all admit to experiencing sadness and pain at least sometimes, it takes further examination for most of us to perceive the more subtle modes of suffering that shadow even the happiest occasion, whether it is just the awareness that the occasion must come to an end, or the persistent intrusion of minor irritations. Usually whatever we do is in constant need of adjustment: for example, either we are too cold or too hot, or we are hungry or stuffed. Wherever we are and whatever we're doing, our body or our mind is uneasy or uncomfortable in some respect, at some level.

In Buddhist doctrine, suffering is classified into three root sections and eight branches. The three root sections are: 1) the suffering of change; 2) pervasive suffering; and 3) the suffering of suffering itself. The eight branches are: 1) birth; 2) sickness; 3) old age; 4) death; 5) unfulfilled desire; 6) unexpected misfortune; 7) separation from loved ones; and 8) physical discomfort.

2) **The Cause of Suffering.** The Second Noble Truth is called *kunjung* (*kun-byung*) in Tibetan, meaning the "source of everything." The source of all suffering is the collaboration between ignorance and karma. Suffering has karmic causes which we accumulate by our own activities performed in ignorance.

3) **The Truth of Cessation.** The Third Noble Truth, *gogpa* ('*gog-pa*) in Tibetan, is the cessation which brings freedom from suffering and the cause of suffering. It is also known as the state of extinguishment, ultimate joy, peace and relaxation, and nirvāṇa.

4) **The Cause of Cessation.** The Fourth Noble Truth, *lam* (*lam*), is the eight-fold path[3] itself, which brings about nirvāṇa.

These are the Four Noble Truths. On the relative level they really exist, and therefore it is necessary for us to understand them fully. Using the metaphor of sickness, we can say that the First Noble Truth diagnoses a disease. If you want to cure a disease, you must discover its cause, the Second Noble Truth. Once you know the cause, your doctor can prescribe treatment: the Buddha is the doctor who is prescribing the path of Dharma. The Dharma path, the Fourth Noble Truth, is like the medicine which will bring you to the state of complete health, the Third Noble Truth of cessation.

From the viewpoint of the absolute truth, these Noble Truths have no more inherent existence than the phenomena we have discussed so far. They are based in great emptiness.

Now Avalokiteshvara, having pronounced the emptiness of both the ground and the path, arrives at the fruit, or goal of our practice: wisdom. This too, is empty of inherent existence.

---

[3] The eight-fold path: 1) right view; 2) right realization; 3) right speech; 4) right conduct; 5) right livelihood; 6) right effort; 7) right mindfulness; (8) right concentration.

"... no wisdom, no attainment, and no non-attainment.
Therefore, Shāriputra, since bodhisattvas have nothing to
attain, they abide in reliance upon Prajñāpāramitā.
Without obscurations of mind, they have no fear.
Completely transcending false views,
they go to the ultimate of nirvāṇa."

There is a stage many practitioners reach of being subtly attached to the state of wisdom itself. It is important for them to cut through such dualistic concepts as wisdom and ignorance, gaining and losing, and attaining enlightenment, if they are to be truly free. The ultimate view is expressed philosophically as "neither ground, path, and fruit, nor no ground, no path, and no fruit."

We must try to understand this point. Both saṃsāra and nirvāṇa are in one single state of great emptiness. Emptiness does not describe just one portion of reality, it is the real nature of every phenomenon whether saṃsāric or nirvānic. There is nothing we can ever grab hold of and cling to forever. We must be brave as regards the true nature, but it takes time to build up the requisite understanding and courage. If we think "Oh, it can't be like that," it means we are hesitating. We are deeply frightened by the true nature. With vajra bravery[4] we can reach the state of total equanimity in all situations. There is neither hope nor fear, neither demons nor gods. This is the ultimate level of fearlessness.

The true way that we exist is the way the reflection of the moon in water exists, and the true way we experience is the way the dreamer experiences. As we either struggle through our dreams or enjoy them, we do so on the assumption that what is happening is real and true in an absolute sense. But it is true only from the context of that dream. When we awaken, where has the situation gone? The people, trees, mountains we just experienced were just an illusion, based on emptiness.

---

[4] Vajra bravery: Diamond-like, indestructible courage.

This dream state is in fact very close to our everyday wakened state. We think we have awakened from a dream into a more real "reality," but in fact, as we pass from sleeping to waking we have simply shifted from one dreamlike state to another. Our waking perceptions are all merely the result of mental habits and karmic patterns accumulated over infinite lifetimes. It is terrifying when we are shaken from the illusory security of such habits. We are afraid to see things differently, and we must give up a lot to do so. When we succeed in changing these patterns, however, our perceptions will be enriched by greater dimensionality, greater understanding and clarity.

**"All the Buddhas of the Three Times awaken completely
to the perfect, unsurpassable enlightenment
by relying on the Prajñāpāramitā."**

Without fear or obscurations, without the slightest concept about their meditative states, the buddhas of the past, present, and future apply these Prajñāpāramitā practices and realize perfect enlightenment. There is no other method except this for doing so.

THE MANTRA

**"Therefore, the mantra of Prajñāpāramitā is the mantra
of great awareness; it is the unsurpassed mantra,
the mantra that equalizes whatever is unequal,
and the mantra that totally pacifies all suffering.
Since it does not deceive, it should be known as truth."**

The term mantra is composed of the two Sanskrit words *man* and *tra*, meaning "mind-protection," or that which protects the mindstream. What it protects from are the negative intellectual and emotional states due to ignorance and grasping.

1) The mantra of Prajñāpāramitā. It will lead to the ultimate destination of enlightenment.

2) The mantra of great awareness. It transforms beginningless darkness into the state of great awareness.

3) The unsurpassed mantra. It introduces us to the profound state of the true nature. There is no higher state than this.

4) The mantra that equalizes whatever is unequal. It brings all of saṃsāra and nirvāṇa into the state of the unsurpassed true nature. The state of equanimity, or state of buddhahood, is known as the state without equal.

5) The mantra that calms all suffering. Prajñāpāramitā calms all suffering by cutting the ego clinging at the root of cyclic existence.

If we practice Prajñāpāramitā along with the recitation of the mantra, we will be able to traverse the five paths of 1) accumulation; 2) application; 3) seeing; 4) meditation; and 5) no more learning. The five paths to enlightenment have been implicit in the unfolding of Avalokiteshvara's exposition on emptiness; also, they are indicated by the five descriptive titles of the mantra above; and finally, they correspond to the words of the mantra, which lead unerringly to the other shore.

"The Prajñāpāramitā mantra is uttered thus:

Tadyathā Om Gate Gate Paragate Parasaṃgate Bodhi Svāhā"

Tadyathā means "thus."

Om has many meanings, but here it means "auspicious," "be strong," and "supreme accomplishment."

Gate means "gone." This first "gate" represents the first willingness of ordinary beings to enter the first path towards enlightenment, the Path of Accumulation.

Gate the second time indicates the readiness of practitioners to advance to the second path, the Path of Application.

Paragate means "supremely gone." It indicates the advance of those on the Path of Application to the Path of Seeing, the third path. This is the first bhūmi, or stage of realization, at which the practitioner has gained freedom from karmic birth in saṃsāra.

Parasaṃgate means "the supremely perfect going." The fourth Path of Meditation covers everyone on the second to tenth bhūmis. It is the path on which the practitioner gains stability in the great, open, vast equanimity, the threshold of enlightenment.

Bodhi means "enlightenment." The Fifth Path of No More Learning, also the eleventh bhūmi, is the state where all realizations are fully accomplished. After following the four paths and the ten bhūmis, there is nothing more to know, no higher levels to attain.

Svāhā means "so be it," or "it is established."

"Shāriputra, it is in this way that bodhisattva mahāsattvas should train in the profound Prajñāpāramitā."

In this, Avalokiteshvara's final statement, he offers encouragement to Shāriputra. All bodhisattvas wishing to attain the state of non-returner must practice according to the profound transcendent knowledge, which breaks down all conceptualization and ego-clinging in the ground of saṃsāra and nirvāṇa.

> "Then the Blessed One arose from that samādhi and praised noble Avalokiteshvara, the bodhisattva mahāsattva, saying: "Good, good, O son of noble lineage! Thus it is, thus it is! One should practice the profound Prajñāpāramitā exactly as you have taught it, and all the Tathāgatas will rejoice!" When the Blessed One spoke these words, venerable Shāriputra and noble Avalokiteshvara, the bodhisattva mahāsattva, together with the whole assembly, and the world with its gods, humans, asuras and gandharvas, all rejoiced, praising what the Blessed One had said."

Here there is universal rejoicing in the Buddha's profound message which benefits all beings without exception. In this essential teaching on the true nature, all beings are considered equal, and in the expanded Prajñāpāramitā teachings, beings are trained in the six pāramitās which foster truth, honesty, love, and non-violence in dealing with one another. All beings possess the buddha nature, a precious treasure as yet undiscovered, which they can finally recognize by cultivating wisdom and compassion on the path. This is cause for rejoicing.

The Buddha, arising from his samādhi, offers the praise and encouragement of the buddhas of the three times and ten directions for all those endeavoring to practice the Prajñāpāramitā. Furthermore, he expresses his own appreciation for the flawless efforts of Avalokiteshvara and Shāriputra.

Ordinarily, it would be disrespectful of students to carry on a discussion while their teacher is deep in meditation. Here, however, the Buddha reveals that he was both aware of and participating in all the aspects of their dialogue. In the Vajrayāna tradition, such an event is called a "mind-to-mind transmission," in which the primacy of meditation over philosophical argument, as a means to understanding, is realized. It was the force of the Buddha's great wisdom and clarity that empowered his disciples to make their discovery, such that the meditation and the discussion were not different manifestations. At the Buddha's level, there is no distinction between meditative and post-meditative states, and in the Vajrayāna, discovery happens first through meditation.

The practice of reciting mantras is not very common in Sūtrayāna practices, to which *The Heart Sūtra* belongs. It is taught extensively, however, in tantra, or the Vajrayāna, which has the same view, meditation and understanding of the true nature of phenomena. The difference between Vajrayāna and Sūtrayāna, and the factor which distinguishes the Vajrayāna from all other forms of Buddhism, lies in the methods of practice, or what are called skillful means. These skillful means, or techniques, are praised as having four qualities. They are: 1) many in number; 2) presented clearly and in detail; 3) easy to perform; and 4) designed for persons with sharp faculties. Therefore, to study and practice the Prajñāpāramita using the skillful means of the Vajrayāna is the most powerful and direct way to gain realization.

This ends my commentary on *The Heart Sūtra*.

QUESTIONS AND ANSWERS

Q: If the natural state of mind is emptiness but yet we exist in a world that is of the aggregates, in order to move through this world and to accomplish things, does that mean that we have to go from the natural state of emptiness back into the states of the aggregates? Can you have speech, action and those things in the natural state of emptiness?

A: The world of the aggregates, as we have just learned, is not a different world from the natural state of emptiness. The great masters are able to perceive this without any going back and forth between two imagined states. But our own perceptions are still completely driven by habit patterns that solidify objects on the relative level. It is only through years of practice that we can reach the point of perceiving relative reality as it really exists: that is, according to the famous saying, "the reflection of the moon in water," or "like a mirage." Another way of describing it is "like a movie." The movie may be beautiful or scary, fun to watch or disturbing; while we are watching it, our emotions and intellect are completely engaged as if everything in the movie were really happening to us. Yet despite this, we know the greater reality that it is only an illusion, a play of celluloid and light. The whole thing depends upon our willingness to ignore the technological fabrication of time and motion. In the same way, the great masters are able to view the comings and going of the aggregates on the relative plane of existence.

Q: When we speak of the appearance of reality as being similar to the reflection of the moon in water, are we implying that there is a greater reality which is the actual moon, not its reflection? Are there times when we are actually perceiving the absolute truth directly like looking straight at the moon in the sky?

A: The metaphor of the reflection of the moon in water should not be elaborated any further with logic. Its meaning is that the absolute reality can be perceived in the reflection itself; this is the ultimate way that even the so-called real moon in the sky exists. So in looking at the moon in the water we are seeing the nature of phenomena exactly. If you try to find some actual moon there on the surface of the water, in the middle or bottom of the pond, you will not. So the reflection is the very point of the metaphor, not the moon itself. We must investigate the way things appear to us, just as a monkey will look behind a mirror to investigate his own reflection. He finds nothing there, no second monkey. In a more abstract example, we can analyze our belief that this is July. But where is July? It is merely a name we have attached to an idea. The right answer to where is July would be to point to our head. That is the reflection of the moon in water. We experience everything according to how we perceive it.

Because the great masters experience this illusory nature of the phenomenal world directly, they also interact with it on that basis. They can walk through walls or suspend themselves in space. These are not abnormal or "fantastic" activities, but rather simply what are called "natural activities." They are the result of perceiving reality exactly as it is, without distinctions.

Q: I want to see if I interpreted you correctly. I always thought that emptiness was like a thing and it sounds like it's not. When we talk about emptiness, we are describing the nature of reality.

A: That's true. Emptiness is not a thing, and cannot be considered separately from phenomena; nor can it be qualified in any way whatsoever. Its qualitylessness cannot be understood within the limits of our ordinary minds, its changelessness under conditions and circumstances is primordially free from any influence. But, for now, a really good theoretical understanding, though not really accurate, is a starting point which will definitely lead us in the direction of true understanding. Only by transcending all subject/ object methods of knowing can this preliminary understanding become the primordial wisdom which sees the true nature directly. Only primordial wisdom has this capacity, and it does this by recognizing itself as identical with the great emptiness.

Q: You have said all things are impermanent, and yet you spoke of the natural state as being "unceasing, doesn't increase or decrease." How can it be both impermanent and not decrease?

A: The things which are impermanent exist only at the relative level, whereas unceasing and unborn refer only to the absolute level. Rather than to say that this unborn absolute state is permanent, it is more accurate to say that it is altogether beyond dualistic terminology, the territory of mundane thought. Our mental formations process works by contradistinction and contrast, producing extreme arguments such as "If it is this, it cannot be that, if it is that, it cannot be this" in a tireless cycle. Words such as impermanent and permanent should simply be considered tools used by the Buddha to communicate the profound nature to ordinary people. In reality the absolute truth goes beyond all this.

Q: We can't realize emptiness through our conceptual minds. So it seems to me we have to have faith that it is there. But in emptiness there is nothing, so that means there is no faith. It seems we have to get to the nature of emptiness through something that's not there. It's hard for me to understand.

A: That's true. First, you must establish the view with your relative awareness. If you continue to meditate and have faith, you are going to realize what is not. The realization of buddhahood is not a solid object we are going to get. Enlightenment is freedom from obscurations and dualistic mental formations. It is total freedom from the mundane. Reality is not something solidly existing and yet is has all good qualities like loving-kindness, compassion, and wisdom. The nature of each of these is emptiness, or, as it is sometimes called, the freedom state.

Q: It seems to me that emptiness has no qualities at all.

A: Emptiness is not a blank state. As Avalokiteshvara said, "Emptiness is form," so it is not just a blank, dark state. It contains the fullness of all qualities. For example, if a rainbow appears, and you run after it in hopes of catching it, will you be able to catch the rainbow? Of course not, and yet there is a rainbow. There are other similes, like the reflection of the moon in water. In the Mahāyāna teachings, Buddha admonishes us not to ignore the qualities of mind, the qualities of emptiness. Therefore in meditation we need to focus on profound emptiness, or the nongrasping, nondual state, but during the post-meditation state, we work with the qualities of the mind like love, compassion, and wisdom. This keeps a balance between the absolute and the relative aspects of mind, so that more and more you will discover the truth of both. Emptiness is not a blank state.

II.

THE SIX PĀRAMITĀS

We have just finished discussing *Prajñāpāramitā* both as a body of teachings and as a philosophical view. It is also the term used for actual meditation practice on the view of the absolute nature. Prajñāpāramitā is the sixth practice belonging to what are known in Sanskrit as the six pāramitās, in Tibetan *paroltuchinpa druk*, in English the "six perfections." The term *pāramitā*, as I explained before, means "to the other shore." The six pāramitās are the bridge we must cross from the shore of saṃsāra and delusion to the other shore, the state of enlightenment. They are the principal practices of the bodhisattva.

Most of the time we try to do our practice on a cushion, maintaining our mind in its natural state free of concepts. This is the combined practice of the fifth pāramitā, concentration, with the sixth pāramitā, *prajñā*, or emptiness meditation. It is difficult to do this, however, while we are engaged in the activities of the world. In order to guide the bodhisattva out of the solitude of sitting meditation and into the world to benefit others, the Buddha taught the first three pāramitās: these are post-meditation trainings in actual behavior, based on loving-kindness and compassion. The fourth pāramitā, joyful effort, is considered an essential support to both the post-meditation and the meditation pāramitās alike.

What we do in our post-meditation time—how we treat our friends, relatives, and business acquaintances—all this counts on the path. It is no more than the reflection of our present state of mind. Because our behavior generates further karma and mental confusion, it is most important to gain control over it. All our progress in realizing the absolute nature will be meaningless if we cannot be generous, disciplined, patient, joyful, and undistracted in our dealings with others. Even if we train in just one of these pāramitās for a short time, we will discover immediate positive results in our relationships. The practice of the sixth pāramitā is a purely mental training which we must try to mingle with the other pāramitās; the view of emptiness should always accompany whatever we do. Compassion and emptiness together are the two essential ingredients of the enlightened state.

The six pāramitās are: 1) generosity; 2) self-discipline; 3) patience; 4) joyful effort; 5) concentration; and 6) wisdom. According to traditional teaching methods, each of these is divided into three categories, usually of increasing difficulty. The bodhisattva trains in each one according to his capacity, until he is able to perform all three.

1. Generosity

ཨྰྀ ཤ(ལ་ཞ་ག(ཤ(ཐ(ཞ(ཞ(ཊ་གྱ(ལ(ཀ(
ཚ(ཧ(ཇ(ག(ལ(ཐ(ཉ(ཐ(ལ(ཕ(ཐ(ལ(ཐ(ཞ(ཐ(ལ(ལ(
སྐ(ཚ(ཞ(ཧ(ཐ(ཚ(ཐ(ལ(ཐ(ལ(ཉ(ཧ(ལ(ཕ(ཉ(ཐ(ལ(ཞ(ཉ(
སྐ(ཉ(ལ(ཞ(ལ(ཐ(ཕ(ལ(ཐ(ཉ(ཉ(ལ(ཉ(ཐ(ཉ(ཐ(ཉ(ཆ(

To whomsoever, whatever is needed, the generosity of wealth;
To those seeking the Dharma, the generosity of excellent teaching;
To those with various fears, the generosity of protection;
May one always be able to afford these three kinds of generosity.

Poem: Treng Go Terchen Sherab Özer
Calligraphy: Khenpo Tsewang Dongyal Rinpoche

When we are generous we give freely, without thought of return. The act of giving out is an antidote to all forms of miserliness, clinging, and poverty. Whether we are sharing material possessions or simply opening up our hearts to others, we are exhibiting an attitude of inner wealth. We are not small, petty, or scheming for our own material profit or egotistical gains.

The three categories of generosity are: a) to give knowledge; b) to give material things; c) to give protection.

a) To give knowledge means to pass on to others whatever skills or wisdom you have learned. This mainly refers to teaching the dharma, if you are qualified, but whatever your area of knowledge is, you offer it freely and openly without pride or ego-cling-

---

Generosity—in Sanskrit, *danā*, in Tibetan, *jimpa* (*sbyin-pa*).

ing. Giving knowledge is like giving light—it removes the darkness of ignorance.

b) To give up your wealth or material possessions is to release your attachment to your own welfare. You are able to see beyond the narrow scope of your own needs and extend care and concern to the needs of others. You try to lessen their poverty by whatever means in your possession. The generosity of wealth can be further subdivided into small, medium and great degrees. You start by giving something small—a penny or a quarter, a fruit, a flower, whatever you can. The medium level would be a gift of something much more important to you—your house or land, for instance. Finally, the great level would be to give up your most cherished possession, your life, to benefit others. Buddha Shākyamuni, for example, gave his life up many times during his previous lives as a bodhisattva.

c) To give protection is to help extend the life of another sentient being, be it a small insect or a human being. This again is done without the slightest expectation of reward or attachment to your own virtuousness.

2. Self-Discipline

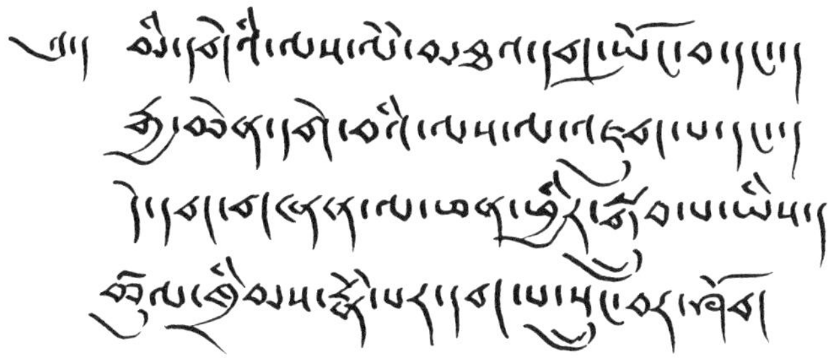

ᠴᠠ᠋ ᠡᡳᠨᡳᡳᠳᡳᠷᠤᠮᠠᠷᡝᡳᠡᠵᠵᠷᠨᠷᠣᡡᠷᡡᠯᠡᠷᡣᠶᡝᡳᠶᠠᡳ
ᠭᡳᠡᠴᠴᠴᡳᡳᠷᡝᡳᡳᠷᡝᡳᠷᠤ� ᠮᠠᡝᠳᠨᠬᠠᠷᠭᡳᠷᠢᠶᡝᠶᡳᡳ
ᠵᡳᠶᠠᡳᡠᡝᡳᠴᠡᠷᡤᠷᠷᠤᠤᡠᠷᠷᡝᡳᠷᠵᠷᠷᡝᠶᡡᠷᠨ
ᡝᠷᠷᠤᠤᠵᠡᠷᠷᡝᠷᠵᠷᠶᡝᠷᡝᠷ

Totally abandoning the highways and byways of unvirtuous activities;
Entering the vast sphere of virtuous activities;
Performing all this for the benefit of others;
May one always be able to maintain perfect discipline!

Poem: Treng Go Terchen Sherab Özer
Calligraphy: Khenpo Tsewang Dongyal Rinpoche

Shīla means "to make correct, to behave ethically," as well as "to discipline oneself." To train in discipline we choose our direction according to right and wrong, and we abandon our wild and negative actions in favor of gentle and positive ones. With the second pāramitā we discipline the total expression of our body, speech, and mind.

The three categores of discipline are: a) discipline that rejects negative actions; b) discipline that accepts positive actions; c) discipline that benefits all sentient beings.

a) All negativity and virtue is classified into actions of the body, speech, and mind. Examples of negative actions of body are to beat or strike others, rob them or take their things without permission, and abuse them sexually. Negative actions of speech are

---

Self-Discipline—in Sanskrit, *shīla*, in Tibetan, *tsultrim* (*tshul-khrims*).

to lie, speak harshly, slander others, and cause divisions between people through words. Negative actions of mind are such emotions as jealousy, anger, pride and so on.

b) The positive actions or virtues are the opposites of those negative actions just described. Any activity based upon compassion, loving-kindness and honesty is positive, no matter how small it may seem at first.

c) Whereas the first two trainings in discipline are directed towards oneself, the third is the training in disciplined effort on behalf of others. As a bodhisattva you are committed to benefit others without discrimination or hesitation, and to always be motivated by honesty and kindness.

3. Patience

ཨ། ན(ཀྱི་བྱེ་རྣམ་ལ་སྙིང་རྗེ་འ་རྗེ་བ་ཡི་ཡི།
སྣ་བ་བྱེ་ར་བ་ཕ་འདུས་ཡི་ལ་ནག་ཡ་ཡི་ཡི།
སྣ་བ་བྱེ་བ་ཟ་བ་ཅ་ནི་ད་གུ་ལ་ཅ་བ་ག་ཡི་ནི།
ཟ་བ་བ་ག་བ་ཟ་བ་ལ་བྱ་ཅ་ལ་ཡི་ལ་བྱ་བྱ་ག་ར་ན།

Generating compassion for all harmdoers;
Joyfully adopting ascetic practice for the Dharma;
Not fearing the ultimate meaning of the profound true nature;
May one always have the ability to practice the greatly worthwhile
    patience.

                Poem: Treng Go Terchen Sherab Özer
            Calligraphy: Khenpo Tsewang Dongyal Rinpoche

The third pāramitā trains us to be steady and open-hearted in the face of difficult people and circumstances. The perfection of patience is the cultivation of skillful courageousness, mindfulness, and tolerance. Usually, when we feel others are hurting or inconveniencing us, we react with various forms of anger and irritation, seeking instantly to strike back. With the pāramitā of patience, however, we remain unwavering as a mountain, neither seeking revenge nor harboring deep resentments inside our hearts. Patient tolerance is the powerful antidote to anger.

    The three categories of patience are: a) patience with enemies; b) patience with the hardships of the path; c) patience with the ups and downs of life.

Patience—in Sanskrit, *kṣanti,* in Tibetan, *zöpa (bzod-pa)*

a) Here we must learn to tolerate all three types of enemies: those who are stronger, those who are weaker, and those who are equally strong as ourselves. Thus, towards those we cannot overcome we avoid harboring jealousy or resentment, towards those we can overcome we avoid cruelty, and with our equals we avoid endless competition or squabbling.

b) Often, no matter how faithfully we perform all the practices of the dharma path, we feel we have achieved nothing. We are so focused on the idea of gain, the goal of enlightenment, that we become discouraged, frustrated, and tired when we begin to realize the difficulty of its actual attainment. To cultivate the patience to eventually reach enlightenment, we focus instead on compassion towards others, while continuing to perform our practices without expectation of immediate results.

c) Third, we must train in having patience with whatever circumstances arise during the course of our lives. Whatever difficulties we encounter should always be considered a very important part of the path. Such ups and downs are inevitable in saṃsāra, and if we can understand them to be manifestations of our own karma which are, in essence, no different from our experiences on the cushion, then we need not be shaken or overwhelmed by them any more than we are by the movements of our own thoughts. In order to remain firmly on the path to enlightenment, we continue patiently on, facing the responsibilities of this life with spiritual dignity and courage of heart.

4. Joyful Effort

ཨ༑། རྒྱལ་འི་གུ་ཤེ་རྣལ་བྱེ་རེ་ནི་ས་བསྱི་ཀུ།
ཇི་འཕྱི་གུ་རྗེ་རེ་ས་ས་མི་ཀུ་ཧ་ན་རྟག་ས་བ་ཀུ།
སྱ་སྱི་འི་ས་རྒྱ་ས་ཧ་ཚེ་ས་ཧྱེ་ཧ་ལེ་ས་བ་ཨི་ཀུ།
རེ་ག་ས་ཚ་གུ་ཤེ་ས་ནི་ས་རྩེ་གུ་ཧ་ས་ཧུ་ཚེ་ས་བར་ས་རྔེ་ས།

The armor which has tremendous joy towards positive activities;
Likewise engaging with intention and application focused;
Not discouraged, unshaken, not prejudiced;
May one always be able to perform joyful effort for what is positive,
day and night.

> *Poem: Treng Go Terchen Sherab Özer*
> *Calligraphy: Khenpo Tsewang Dongyal Rinpoche*

To combat all modes of laziness and self-satisfaction, we train in the pāramitā of joyful effort. *Vīrya* is the kind of effort that is ongoing, diligent, enthusiastic, and dedicated to the wellbeing of others. With *vīrya* the bodhisattva cultivates the energy necessary to care for limitless sentient beings.

The three categories of effort are: a) unflinching courage; b) insatiable effort; c) unceasing effort.

a) Unflinching courage is necessary in order to confront the immensity of the bodhisattva's task. Sentient beings are infinite, countless; as soon as you have helped one, another comes along. After hundreds have come and gone, thousands are still waiting.

Joyful Effort—in Sanskrit, *vīrya*, in Tibetan, *tsöndru* (*brtson-'grus*).

Your joyful effort must extend to each one of them without becoming overwhelmed and discouraged.

b) Often when we achieve even the slightest spiritual realization, or when we manage to help just a few other beings, we feel we have done enough and are quite self-satisfied. It is said, however, that the only thing we should feel satiated by is the extent of our negative actions. Until all beings have been brought to the state of complete enlightenment, we must exert ourselves with energy that is never diminished by satisfaction.

c) If we have unflinching courage and diligence that is never satisfied, we will work night and day to accomplish the benefit of all sentient beings; our effort will be enthusiastic, joyful, and unceasing.

5. Concentration

ཨཿ ཨ༷ཐི(འྀ'ཟཡ'ཆེ'ཆེ'དྷི'ར(ཨ༷)'(ཟར(ཟ)(ཟ)ཡཡ(ཟ)(༷(༷)

ཝེ'ཟཉ(ར)(ཟ)ཇཱ(ར(ཟཝཉ(ཟ)ཟ(ཟ)(ཧོ)ཇཱ(ཟ)ཆྀ(༷)(ར)(༷(༷)

ཟ(ཟ)(ཟ)(ཟ)ཡ(ར)ཟ(ཟ)ཟེ(ཟ)(ར)(ཆི)ཟ(ཧྀ)ཟ(ཟ)ཟ(ར)(ར)(ཟ)ཉེ(༷)

ཟཕ(ར)(ཇ)ཇཱ(ཟཾ)(ཟ)(ར)ཡ(ཟ)ཟ(ཟེ)ཟ(ཟ)ཡ(ར)ཟ(ཐི)ཟ(ཟ)(ར)(ཟཉེ)(ཟ)

During the time of a peaceful and joyful life in the state of direct
perception;
Gradually increasing the great qualities;
Performing beneficial works for others through clearly understanding
their natures;
May one always be able to preserve in equanimity the meaning
of perfect concentration.

Poem: Treng Go Terchen Sherab Özer
Calligraphy: Khenpo Tsewang Dongyal Rinpoche

Dhyāna means to maintain the mind in an even, calm state. By training in the fifth pāramitā, we gain control over our minds. At present, our minds are very unstable, very wild. The signs that people do not control their minds are easily visible around us: craziness; chronic upsetness, sadness, depression; distractedness; compulsions, tantrums and hyperactivity. With concentration, we cultivate the power to bring our minds into a state of clarity and equanimity. We can become happier, more delightful to others, and more insightful. It is most important for us to tame our minds now.

Concentration—in Sanskrit, *dhyāna*, in Tibetan, *samten* (*bsam-gtan*).

The three categories of concentration are: a) worldly concentration; b) concentration that goes beyond the world; c) concentration that benefits others.

a) Worldly concentration is called the first stage of concentration. We train our minds simply to relax and rest in one-pointed evenness. There is no realization of love and compassion, emptiness and egolessness. We achieve a temporary peace.

b) This is called the supreme concentration. It is based upon bodhicitta; in it we experience compassion for all sentient beings and we understand the true nature, without ego-clinging or dualistic thoughts. Our minds are totally free from all mental fabrications. It is the natural state, like deep space or the sky.

c) Having attained the realization of the supreme concentration, we have the capacity to benefit others. This is the concentration that extends to others.

6. Supreme Wisdom

ཨ༔ ག་ཏེ་ཆོ་ཅུ་ལ་ཅུ་ལུ་ར་ནེ་ཧ་ལ་ལི་ག།
ཁ་ི་ལྷ་ཧ་ུ་ལ་ཅ་ཛ་ཐ་ན་ཅུ་ར་ནོ་ཧ་ལ་ཀ་ལྲ།
ཤུ་ལུ་ར་ལ་ཆུ་ཀ་ག་ཉ་ཙོ་ལ་ཀྲུ་ཅ་ལ་ཅ་ཧ་ལ་ལི་ག།
ཙེ་ཧ་ལ་ཧི་ཙོ་ཅ་ལ་ཅ་ནེ་ཧ་ར་ཆ་ལྱ་གི་ལུ་ར་ནེན།

Understanding clearly all of relative truth as mirage;
Realizing the absolute truth as the sky, free from all complexities;
In particular, having the expertise to complete the beneficial works for
   others;
May one always possess the perfect wisdom of hearing, contemplation,
   and meditation.

Poem: Treng Go Terchen Sherab Özer
Calligraphy: Khenpo Tsewang Dongyal Rinpoche

Pra means "supreme, primordial," or "pure"; *jña* means "wisdom." Supreme, transcendental wisdom is the antidote to all dualistic thinking contrived in ignorance. When we train in wisdom we are developing the ability to see with clear, open, unerring and undistorted vision. We will gradually gain understanding of the true nature of reality in both its relative and absolute aspects.

The three categories of prajñā are called, in Tibetan, *thopa* (*thos-pa*), *sampa* (*bsam-pa*), and *gompa* (*sgom-pa*). They refer to the wisdoms that come from: a) hearing, or study; b) contemplation, or understanding; and c) meditation, or total integration.

Supreme Wisdom—in Sanskrit, *prajñā*, in Tibetan, *sherab* (*shes-rab*).

a) The great Tibetan institutes of learning used to teach ten fields of knowledge: these were the five major and the five minor sciences. I think that all knowledge, including the modern technologies, still can be represented in these ten categories. The first stage of wisdom is called "hearing" because Tibetans learned mostly through lectures and memorization rather than through studying books. When we hear—or study—these sciences, we gain the knowledge of many facts and skills. Knowing things at their technical—or superficial level—is the first necessary stage of wisdom.

b) It is not enough to gain knowledge simply from reading books or hearing instructions; we will be able to repeat facts and formulas and perform tasks mechanically, but will we understand the meaning? We must deepen our understanding by contemplating thoroughly what we have read and heard. This stage of wisdom arrived at through contemplation is very clear and certain: it is called certainty wisdom, from the Tibetan term *ngeshe* (*nges-shes*). It is very important to reach the level of certainty wisdom in all the areas of our lives. Otherwise we will be allowing our minds to rest in states of subtle confusion, denying ourselves the success and fulfillment of lessons truly learned.

When we contemplate successfully, we do not simply accept what has been taught. We use our intellect to analyze over and over again, until we feel certain that our projections, exaggerations, and fantasies have been eliminated. We are really trying to discover exactly what is; to do this, we must constantly refer to what we have learned about the absolute nature, keeping our minds clear of the extremes of nihilism and eternalism.

There are several methods of correct contemplation, which we practice according to our capacities. First, however, it is necessary to turn inward; then we can proceed via either the dualistic methods of logic and inference, or via actual direct perception. These methods must be practiced not once but many times, over and over again, if we wish to secure the wisdom of complete certainty.

c) The certainty wisdom which will arise in our minds as a result of the first two disciplines of study and contemplation is still an awareness limited by the dualism of intellect. We have yet to reach the third wisdom of actual experience and realization. This third wisdom is the wisdom of the third eye, or enlightenment. The method of cultivating this final level of awareness is a subtle process of integration within the meditative state. Only by means of meditation, rather than study, can we mingle the immediate experiences of mind with the knowledge and skills gained in the preliminary steps of developing prajñā. Meanings and insights which have matured in our awareness will increase in clarity and profundity; there will be a radical alteration of consciousness, which is experienced in the form of light. The stages of this wisdom developed in *gom*, or meditation, are defined as: 1) understanding; 2) experience; and 3) realization, or enlightenment.

This concludes the teaching on the six pāramitās. Whoever has taken the bodhisattva vow must take these practices to heart. Whether or not we call such a practitioner "bodhisattva" is not important; the true bodhisattva is the one who actually practices the six pāramitās. Regardless of name, he or she will inexorably cross the bridge to enlightenment.

During the beginning it is important to focus on your successes rather than your failures. With repeated practice, your mind and wisdom will open up and your capabilities will increase. It is important to begin by taking the pāramitās individually, for short periods, and applying them to daily life, in the office and the home. You can concentrate on whichever pāramitā seems most relevant to how you are feeling; for example, if you have trouble giving, you would meditate on generosity.

Meditation and practice have the power to bring a tremendous inner joy which surpasses all others. The joy of parties and picnics, for example, is temporary and goes as soon as they are over. The joy from meditation and practice, however, brings benefits to yourself and others which are limitless, because it is a joy revealed from the deep nature of mind. The extent of joy in your heart and the joy you bring to others will always be dependent upon the extent to which your mind is motivated by loving-kindness and compassion. This is the point of view shared by all human beings, not just dharma practitioners. It is the most important standard by which we all judge one another. It is the essential practice of dharma as taught by the buddhas. Compassion and loving-kindness, based upon emptiness—that is the condensed heart practice of the Prajñāpāramitā.

DEDICATION

By this stainless merit, the heavy darkness of sentient beings will be removed. It will radiate the true wisdom light of the sun and the moon, making bloom the lotus garden of joy and peace for all sentient beings.

APPENDIX I

THE TEN MENTAL DISTRACTIONS WHICH ARE ELIMINATED THROUGH THE TEACHING OF THE PRAJÑĀPĀRAMITĀ

1. The conception of a self.
2. The conception of the lack of a self.
3. Conceptions about the self that are not true.
4. Failure to recognize the proper characteristics of the self.
5. The conception of the self as one.
6. The conception of the self as many.
7. The conception of the self as more than just a name.
8. The conception of the self as having characteristics.
9. The conception of the self according to name.
10. The conception of the self according to meaning.
    (*i.e.,* my name is Lotus, therefore I am really a lotus.)

APPENDIX II

THE SIXTEEN CLASSIFICATIONS OF EMPTINESS

The sixteen emptinesses are presented by the Buddha to facilitate the understanding that all phenomenal existence, no matter how complex, is empty. A further four emptinesses detail the emptiness of all distinctions in general, expressing the meaning in a more concise, abstract way.

1. The emptiness of external objects. The six outer objects of perception are empty by nature.
2. The emptiness of internal subjects. The six inner sources of perception are empty by nature.
3. The emptiness of what is both external and internal. Examples of this are the gross physical bases of the senses; whatever is neither subject nor object.
4. The emptiness of emptiness. Emptiness itself is non-existent.
5. The emptiness of the great. The ten directions and space are the vast, all-pervading expanse of emptiness.
6. The emptiness of the ultimate. The state of enlightenment, the absolute truth itself, is also empty of any inherent existence.
7. The emptiness of the compounded. All things having parts, birth, and cessation are empty.

8. The emptiness of the uncompounded. All things without parts or an existence within time, such as space, are empty in nature.

9. The emptiness of that which is beyond extremes. Whatever is free from the extremes of eternalism and nihilism, and from all opposites, is empty by nature.

10. The emptiness of that which has neither beginning nor end. Saṃsāra is said to be without beginning or end because a decisive moment of its creation and final moment of its cessation cannot be found. Being uncreated, it is empty by nature.

11. The emptiness of that which is not to be rejected. Even the nature of things we discover we cannot change or reject is empty. Rejection and non-rejection do not happen.

12. The emptiness of the self-nature of phenomena. On the absolute level there is nothing, no essence or creator, which makes things the way they are. For example, the heat which is the cause and essence of fire has no inherent existence.

13. The emptiness of all phenomena. Both compounded and uncompounded things are uncreated and empty in nature.

14. The emptiness of characteristics. The qualities, nature, ideas, and concepts which define things, whether subject or object, samsāra or nirvāna, are all empty in nature.

15. The emptiness of the unapprehensible. An example of what is unapprehensible are the three times, since the past is gone, the present is fleeting, and the future has not yet come. Within the high level of awareness of the non-existence of the three times, objects also disappear. The unapprehensible objects, their unapprehensibility, and the enlightened state which does not apprehend are empty in nature.

16. The emptiness of non-identity. On the ultimate level, no distinction can be made between existence and non-existence. Therefore the absence of any existing identity is also inherently empty in nature.

THE FOUR EMPTINESSES

1. The emptiness of things. All compounded things exist only insofar as they are empty in nature.

2. The emptiness of non-things. All uncompounded things, such as space, are empty.

3. The emptiness of self-nature. On the absolute level, there is no distinction between self and other. The nature of any phenomenon is not exclusive to itself, and cannot be distinguished as anything but empty.

4. The emptiness of other-nature. Things cannot have the nature of another rather than the nature of self.

Appendix III

A SUMMARY IN EIGHT POINTS
OF THE
HIDDEN MEANING
OF THE
PRAJÑĀPĀRAMITĀ TEACHINGS

These eight points are a kind of outline of the contents of the Prajñāpāramitā teachings. The first three points describe the three states of wisdom possessed by a buddha, a bodhisattva, and a shrāvaka/pratyekabuddha, respectively. Points four through seven describe, in oversimplified form, various methods of the path. The eighth point is buddhahood itself.

1. **Sarvajñāna.** Omniscient wisdom. This is the awareness of a buddha which sees all things in their relative and absolute states. Omniscient wisdom dispels the darkness of ignorance, and benefits all sentient beings.
2. **Margajñāna.** Path wisdom. This is the wisdom of the bodhisattva, which knows the causes and conditions that constitute the perfect path towards enlightenment. This perfect path is the cultivation of wisdom and compassion for the benefit of beings.
3. **Vastujñāna.** Basic ground wisdom. This is the wisdom of the pratyekabuddha and shrāvaka, which knows the bases of both

the perfect and imperfect paths and therefore knows what to accept and reject. The basis of the perfect path is wisdom and compassion, and the basis of the imperfect path is the lack of wisdom and compassion.

4. **Sarvākārābhisambodha**. Complete awakening to all aspects of phenomena. This occurs with the thorough application of the skillful means of compassion and the wisdom of emptiness to all phenomenal existence. This is the path of uniting the wisdoms of the first three points.

5. **Mūrdhaprayoga**. Yoga of the peak experience. This is the training in the peak experience immediately preceding the breakthrough to enlightenment.

6. **Anupūrvaprayoga**. Yoga of the successive stages. This is the training in the gradual stages of the path, which occur one after the other in successive order.

7. **Ksanikaprayoga**. Yoga of the moment. This is the training in the experience at the actual moment of enlightenment, when all the stages of the path occur simultaneously.

8. **Phaladharmakāya**. Fruit of the dharmakāya. This is the final attainment of buddhahood, the wisdom truth body.